Shooting the Moon

Shooting the Moon

Brian Willems

zero books

Winchester, UK
Washington, USA

First published by Zero Books, 2015
Zero Books is an imprint of John Hunt Publishing Ltd., Laurel House, Station Approach,
Alresford, Hants, SO24 9JH, UK
office1@jhpbooks.net
www.johnhuntpublishing.com
www.zero-books.net

For distributor details and how to order please visit the 'Ordering' section on our website.

ISBN: 978 1 78279 848 4
Library of Congress Control Number: 2014949210

A CIP catalogue record for this book is available from the British Library.

Design: Stuart Davies

Printed in the USA by Edwards Brothers Malloy

CONTENTS

To Jasna

List of Illustrations

Introduction

The First Men in the Moon (1964)

As soon as you put the moon on screen it is lost. This is equally true for a wide range of moon films, including the theatricality of Méliès, the incredulity of camp, the illegibility of footage shot by Apollo astronauts and the revisionary history of *Transformers 3* (2011). For the moon appears in a quite realistic fashion when seen from a distance, yet when it is viewed from up close all sorts of fantastic things spring forth, from giant mushrooms and nude women to unattributable sounds and killer rocks. On the one hand this observation seems blasé, for the moon has been known to the naked eye for all of humanity's history, while it was only zoomed in on in stages, with the help of Galileo's telescope in the early 17th century, the Soviet Luna flybys of the 1950s, images taken with the help of lunar impact and lander craft, culminating in the recordings of the Apollo 11 crew on the lunar surface in 1969 and finally the more detailed images available today. Yet films centering on the moon can show that even after landing on the moon our nearest celestial neighbor has lost none of its aptitude for being made of green cheese. In fact, in some ways the moon gets even stranger the more of a known entity that it becomes.

Yet the fact that the moon becomes less known the closer we get to it is not disparaging; actually, it a great sign of hope. For, as paradoxical as it might seem at first, it is actually only when we "lose sight" of the moon that lunar truths begin to come forth. Put simply, this is because fantastic elements of the moon indicate, by their mere absurdity, non-fantastic elements. Thus when the lunar surface looks like a theatrical backdrop, or it is populated by Cat-Women or Nazis, what it is showing is that (as Scott Montgomery says of Galileo's descriptions of his telescopic moon) what is really discovered on the moon is the earth.[1] In this sense even when films seem to avoid the moon altogether, such as *Cosmic Voyage* (1936) or *Destination Moon* (1950), they actually have something to say about how the unknown is represented. In early pre-World War II lunar films the technique for representing the unknown is cubist in the nature of its multiple yet concurrent representations, in camp films the technique is one of blatant absurdity, in films made before the lunar landing an attempt to depict the moon as realistically as possible often involves not showing it at all, the technique of actually filming the moon on its surface is seen to be no guarantee of the infallibility of the image, while films made after 1969 deploy many of the earlier techniques of shooting the moon in order to expand the narrative potential of our celestial neighbor.

To illustrate one way that this "lost moon" functions, let's look at three adaptations of H.G. Wells' 1901 novel *The First Men in the Moon*. In the novel Dr Cavor is a turn-of-the-century scientist who has invented Cavortie, a substance which makes objects resistant to gravity, a fact which he exploits to go to the moon, taking his neighbor Bedford along for the ride. The first film adaptation is J.L.V. Leigh's version from 1919, which is appropriately lost itself: it has not been shown since the beginning of 1920 and it is one of the earliest entries on the British Film Institute's list of 75 most wanted films.[2] Yet a well-publicized frame survives, showing a group of theatrically costumed moon-men with bulging brains who would look at home in one of Matthew Barney's *Cremaster* (1994-2002) films.[3] The Moon Men are surrounding Cavor (Hector Abbas), who seems to be trying to explain something to them. It is absurd to posit that anything literally resembling this image was believed to have ever existed on the moon by the filmmaker, for, as a contemporary reviewer of the film complained, "the landscapes of the Moon are too obviously canvas fakes."[4] In other words, its truth obviously lies elsewhere than realism.

This is a lesson lost on the most recent adaptation of the novel, made for BBC Four in 2010. This TV version offers a frame for Wells' story: after the 1969 moon landing, the now elderly Bedford reminisces about having been on the moon first. Thus in an extended flashback the film can show all of the absurdities found in Wells' novel, including the Selenites, moon cows and fields of gold, all of which are destroyed long before the Apollo astronauts make their landing. However, a final shot shows a Selenite observing the Apollo astronauts, although the alien is only seen by the audience. While this would seem to confirm the fantastic elements of Wells' moon, this fantasy is actually negated by the fact that the Selenites are only seen by the extra-diegetic viewer, and therefore the current understanding of the moon as a relatively barren rock remains undisturbed within the content of the film.

The most interesting adaptation is the interstitial one, Nathan Juran's 1964 production, with Lionel Jeffries as Dr Cavor, Edward Judd as Arnold Bedford, and a new lunar passenger, Bedford's fiancée Katherine Callender, played by Martha Hyer. This film also features a framing device: the United Nations launches a lunar mission in 1964. The flight and landing are shown in an attempt at realism, showing how the propulsion system functions and the softness of the lunar surface upon touch-down. However, soon the astronauts discover a British Union Jack and a note attesting that a Dr Cavor claimed the moon for Queen Victoria in 1899. This sets the scene for the discovery of a lunar-crazed Bedford in a sanatorium on Earth and a long flashback showing his fantastic adventures with Dr Cavor, which are full of underground cities, hive-minds, and stop-motion lunar cows that look like big caterpillars. Yet what is most striking about this version is what happens at the end. Returning to the contemporary setting of the frame story, Bedford watches the UN astronauts live on TV as they discover the Selenite city, although it crumbles to dust as they enter it, having long been desolate. (It is assumed that Dr Cavor, who remained on the moon, unintentionally wiped the Selenites out by spreading a common cold he had at the time.) Thus the current understanding of the moon as a desolate satellite is reconfigured: the moon is shown to have contained life, although now extinct, and this knowledge is germane for the characters in the film; in other words, the barrenness of the moon is no longer a sign that life could never be but rather that life once was.

Juran's moon is a figure which is both known, as seen in the realistic depiction of the UN landing, and unknown, as seen in the confirmation of Selenite existence at the end. This fantastic element of the moon indicates a kind of lunar truth in that even pointing the camera directly at the lunar surface, as shown in the UN scenes, is no guarantee of the truth of the lunar image: the moon remains fantastic even when we know better, an idea unfortunately negated by the ending of the BBC adaptation. What is of interest here is not a preference for a realistic or fantastic lunar truth, but rather that the moon is an object which invites, or even demands, more than one truth at once. In other words, when multiple techniques of lunar presentation are used together, a difference, or gap between such presentations comes forth. It is through such a gap that the moon starts to become known, although only in an indirect fashion, for shooting the moon directly is no guarantee of truth. For in the words of Graham Harman, "When it comes to grasping reality, illusion and innuendo are the best we can do."[5] Thus fantastic or camp films can be seen to capture elements of the moon that actual footage shot on its surface lacks. In addition, films made after the moon landings can be seen as reinvigorating these techniques in their appropriations of the moon as a vehicle for understanding.

Part 1: Early Films

Chapter 1

Le Voyage dans la Lune/A Trip to the Moon (1902)

[Blackboard] The first time the moon appears in Georges Méliès' classic *Le Voyage dans la Lune* (1902) it is a small, white circle drawn in chalk on a blackboard. The leader of a group of astronomers, Professor Barbenfouillis (played by Méliès), explains his idea of how to get to the moon; his theory is that a large cannon on the earth will propel a capsule to the lunar surface. The trajectory of the capsule is represented by a slightly convex dotted line, perhaps indicating the pull of the dense gravity of large celestial bodies.[6] At the end of this line the capsule is depicted going "face-first" into the moon, indicating the crash landing that is, strangely enough, shown twice in the film: first in the eye of the Man in the Moon and then again on the fantastic lunar surface.[7] While the moon on the blackboard is depicted as a small white mass (perhaps with the face of the Man in the Moon drawn on it), the earth is different: it has a number of geodesic lines which indicate an understanding of its curvature. Looking like a basketball, these lines point to a number of differences in how the earth and its moon are understood in the film: Earth is an entity which scientific understanding has encircled, while the moon remains a fuzzy blank mass, waiting to be filled with knowledge.

[Telescope] While the blackboard shows an image of a "fuzzy" moon, a prominent prop in the first shot of *Le Voyage* indicates how this fuzziness can be "filled in": a large telescope is pointed out of one of the windows in the background of the astronomy hall, indicating what Marjorie Hope Nicolson calls "the telescopic moon," referring to the shift in literary representations of the moon after Galileo first saw and described the lunar surface with something to aid the human eye.[8] The connection between the moon and the telescope is also made by the composition of the shot. Both the trajectory of the capsule on the blackboard and the body of the telescope point from right to left, going out the window. Thus it could be argued that a comparison is being made: the telescope is a means (like the rocket ship) for seeing the moon more clearly. Or, because the moon had already been observed by telescope for centuries, yet still remains "fuzzy" on the blackboard, the rocket ship is poised to continue where the telescope leaves off, creating a "rocket moon" to replace the "telescopic" one.[9]

[Gun] When the launch of the capsule eventually takes place, the extension of telescopic vision into rocket vision is manifest in the shape of the gun used to fire the bullet-shaped capsule to the lunar surface. The images of the telescope and gun are connected in that both take the form of a diagonal rising from left to right, both are seemingly made from a similar metal, and both have been constructed out of multiple sections. Thus both telescope and gun can be read together as inventions which extend the limited range of humanity's visual power, the former through magnification and the latter through projection. However, as these two inventions are read together an important difference between them comes forth: the shape of the telescope widens, from smaller to bigger, meaning that the eye-piece of the telescope is smaller than the other end, while the shape of the gun tapers, with the end for inserting the capsule into the chamber being "large" and the end aimed at the moon, through foreshortening, being considerably smaller, almost coming to a point. Although the extreme foreshortening of the gun is a part of the film's style (because in a literal sense the barrel would have to be the same size as the chamber in order for the capsule to exit), the image of the gun could be said to form a counter image to the telescope.

This argument can be supported by a more abstract difference between the inventions in the film. The telescope is connected to the fuzzy image of the moon which appears on the blackboard in the astronomers' hall. The astronomers have presumably already used the telescope to observe the moon and what is on the blackboard represents the limited nature of their observations. Therefore, a rocket has been built to improve them. This line of thought is supported by the image of the moon which appears in the launch scene, for it is depicted with a similar "fuzziness" to the moon on the blackboard; thus the rocket is aimed at obliterating a lack of understanding.[10] However, connecting the telescope to limited knowledge and the trip to the moon to improving what is known by direct observation brings forth one of the paradoxes of the film, a paradox which will never quite be absent from the history of the moon on film, for landing on the moon is very often about the *loss* of knowledge. In this sense, as the astronomers get physically closer to the moon they lose sight of it, as seen by the film's (and maybe cinema's as a whole) most famous image—the Man in the Moon. Thus the images of the moon in *Le Voyage* are most accurate when the moon in shown from a distance, although this is a "fuzzy" kind of accuracy. At the same time, the trip to the moon does not resolve this "fuzziness," in fact it increases it.

[Approach] On the one hand it is naïve to state that because for most of its history humanity has known the moon from afar, film presentations of the "far away" moon will be more accurate than the lunar surface seen from up close. However, despite the surface validity of this argument, fictions which take place on the moon often surface a certain kind of truth (and a lot of hooey) that direct observation misses. This truth is due to the fact that because for so long it was impossible to see the moon "up close" multiple strategies for lunar representations had to be developed.

Some of these strategies contain "lunar truths" in themselves. Once humanity landed on the moon the situation did not change; in other words, just because the surface of the moon was recorded from the surface of the moon, this did not mean that the use of multiple representational strategies together came to an end. In fact, it only increased.

The initial example of how such truth gets located in fiction can be see in the approach to the moon, which is shown from the point of view of the capsule coming in for a landing.[11] There are three main elements in the representation of the moon in this scene: at first it is shown in a fuzzy manner, meaning a mainly white disc with a few marks roughly indicating what can be seen with the naked eye from Earth; then, as the capsule approaches, a dissolve replaces the fuzzy moon with one with a visible face; then the capsule is famously shown landing in the Moon Man's right eye.

While in general the progression of these images can be seen as a "loss" of realism, there is also the chance that when taken together they can be read as an *indirect approach* to picturing "lunar truths." This is because getting closer to the moon in the film does not bring about any attempt at showing a "true" moon. Rather, its face is a piece of theatricality (not an attempt by Méliès to show what he thought the surface of the moon really looked like). Yet it is through such theatricality that differences between a fantastic moon and a real moon become more apparent. In other words, the fantastic makes the real more visible because it becomes so apparent that the real is missing. This brings us to a discussion of the role indirectness plays in bringing about a kind of truth that direct observation misses.

[Indirectness] The moon is not just seen in one way but rather it undergoes a number of different presentational strategies. So far, in *Le Voyage* the moon has been put on screen in the following manners: a fuzzy circle on a blackboard; a fuzzy circle in the sky;

and as the face of the Man in the Moon. What will be added to these is of course the actual landscape of the moon seen after landing, which in the case of *Le Voyage* takes the form of a fantastic stage set.

In other words the moon is represented as: a) an unclear scientific drawing; b) an unclear object seen in the night sky by the naked eye; c) an unreal moonscape when seen from close range; and d) a fantastic moonscape when seen from on the ground. This multiplicity of approaches indicates the structural nature of indirect representation: a single object, the moon, is presented through different strategies in the same film, in this case *Le Voyage*. Most important, however, is that this multiple presentation becomes an issue. These multiple strategies actually bring about a tension or conflict between the object of the moon and its own qualities. This was seen above in how the absurd Man in the Moon begins to indicate what the moon actually is (meaning, in the very least, that it is not a literal human face). This approach can be called indirect because the same object is shown in different ways (a-d above) in the same film. When the conflict between different presentations becomes an issue it can indicate some features of an object because, as Graham Harman argues (using a boat as his example), "This forces us to confront the tension between the unified haunted boat and its multitude of shifting features. Let 'confrontation' be the name for those sporadic cases where we come directly to grips with the difference between a thing and its slippery sensual traits."[12]

Although Harman uses a number of terms in this quote which are developed below, here it can be said that he defines a number of different strategies for bringing about such an awareness throughout his work, but there are two which will have the most bearing on *Le Voyage*: a "vertical" strategy and a "horizontal" strategy. The first, in short, brings about a tension between an object as it is used "unthinkingly" in an everyday manner and the real, contorted, always-beyond-our-reach object hiding underneath the surface of everyday use. This gap is "vertical" because it is found between the way an object is experienced and the "real" object that forever lies veiled. In other words, it is present when "real objects forever withdraw behind their accessible, sensual presence to us."[13] In *Le Voyage* this kind of indirectness has been termed "fuzzy."

The other kind of gap Harman denotes is a "horizontal" gap in which the hidden or veiled "real" object does not come in to play; instead, there is a tension between an "everyday" object and its own "everyday" qualities. This can be seen, for example, in a cubist painting where an image of a face is in tension with its cut-up and rearranged image: there is no "real" face involved here, everything takes place on the surface. For Harman this gap exits "between the relatively durable objects of our perception and their swirling kaleidoscope of shifting properties."[14] In *Le Voyage* this strategy has been seen in the multiple presentations of the moon taking place together: in other words, representations of the moon are put into tension with other representations. Horizontal gaps are important because theatrical representations of the moon, through their mere absurdity, have the potential to indirectly, or horizontally, indicate where gaps in lunar understanding lie.

Horizontal confrontations have been noticed in Méliès' work in a number of ways, for what is traditionally called his "magic" (in distinction to Lumièr's realism)[15] actually stands for a gap between fantasy and reality. As André Gaudreault argues, "Méliès' filmic system [...] almost always establishes a relationship between spectators and the screen based on the *recognition* of the cinematic illusion."[16] For Harman, Martin Heidegger is a key figure in this recognition: not only is his thought important in becoming aware of the mechanism of a vertical confrontation of elements but it is also key for understanding the tense gathering of qualities in a horizontal confrontation; thus a brief tour through his thought and some of those who have thought after him becomes necessary.

[Gathering] Heidegger calls the horizontal structure of a confrontation of multiples *das Geviert,* meaning a quad or fourfold, and it plays a key role in "Building Dwelling Thinking," a lecture he gave in 1951. Heidegger names the four elements of his gathering earth, sky, divinities and mortals.[17] However, the details of why each of these terms is important for his thought are not germane here. Rather I am interested in the reason why he thinks that an experience of different elements together can allow for an indirect or horizontal experience of an object.[18] Harman calls this experience a horizontal "confrontation" in that different aspects of an experience of an object are allowed to reside alongside each other in agitation or conflict, just like how the different cubist representations of a face are allowed to remain in conflict with the "everyday" experience of an image of a face. Thus for Harman there is a sense of violence attached to the fourfold. Heidegger, on the other hand, sees this relationship as something more reserved, calling the relationship between the four dwelling [*Wohnen*],[19] indicating a kind of "living-with" rather than a struggling-with. However, the reason Heidegger is being brought in here is that this "fourfold" way of being with an object (through multiple representational strategies, for example) becomes a means of *accessing a kind of truth about the object itself.* One of the tasks for this book is to develop how this happens. While Heidegger calls horizontal tension a "building,"[20] for Harman it is a coming to grips, as quoted above, "with the difference between a thing and its slippery sensual traits."[21]

The difference created by the horizontal tension of multiple representations is a different way of having access to the totality of things: "we are left to encounter a realm of phenomenal presence, entirely different in kind from the underground zone of concealment. Human life is adrift in a sensual realm."[22] This horizontal tension is sensual, meaning it is removed from the real object, yet it is also a kind of "realism" because "Realism does not mean that we are able to state correct propositions about the real world. Instead, it means that reality is too real to be translated without remainder into any sentence, perception, practical action, or anything else."[23] In the context of the films under discussion here, contact with the moon comes about in the way the moon is always more than the presentations of it, a point which is forcefully made with the appearance of different presentational strategies gathered together in the same film.

[Attractions] One way to understand the position of *Le Voyage* in a discussion of a horizontal or indirect approach is to see how this reading of the film is both similar to and different from a "cinema of attractions" as developed by Tom Gunning. His classic essay from 1986, "The Cinema of Attractions: Early Film, Its Spectator and the Avant-Garde," is first and foremost an attempt at reading cinema in a non-narrative manner.[24] Gunning aims at restoring early silent cinema to an "exhibitionist confrontation rather than diegetic absorption."[25] This confrontation is reminiscent of Harman in how it aims at showing the integrity of the multiplicity of elements which make up a film, rather than focusing on their subservience to an overall narrative. This can be seen in Gunning's discussion of close-ups in early cinema, which "differ from later uses of the technique precisely because they do not use enlargement for narrative punctuation, but as an attraction in its own right."[26] However, Gunning's reading of early cinema diverges from an indirect approach in a major way: Gunning insists on a more traditional subject/object relationship when he states that "Every change in film history implies a change in its address to the spectator, and each period constructs its spectator in a new way."[27] While Gunning's comment indicates an important gain in film studies (the work done to create a spectator by the structure of a film), when he locates film and spectator in such a web it denies a place for the object (a film, the moon) to exist apart from its observer.[28] A similar criticism is leveled by Harman against New Historicism: he states that by taking context to be of foremost importance New Historicism is "turning *everything* into an inter-related cosmos of influences."[29] While New Historicism and a Cinema of Attractions are very different beasts, the criticism lodged against them is similar: it is not "enough" to locate a work within a network of influences, instead what needs to be shown is how the multiplicity of a network provides a separation from and thus access to an object. This train of thought can initially be developed through looking at the multiple landings which take place in *Le Voyage*.[30]

[Landings] In *Le Voyage* this kind of "tension" or "confrontation" is seen in the fact that the landing is shown twice, and in two very different manners. This indicates one of the contributions that "filmic moon studies" can offer to a theory of indirect access, because we can map out a number of different ways in which an object is experienced.

The first landing in the eye takes place during the approach, which is mainly shown from the point of view of the capsule. However, when this landing actually takes place the capsule enters the frame, changing the focalization of the scene from that of the capsule to a more objective point of view, or something approaching zero-focalization. In this sense the first landing can be said to contain two points of view of the moon in that we shift from a point of view shot to that of something more objective. However, this objectivity is in tension with the crash of the capsule into the Moon Man's eye, which obviously makes no claims to realism. Yet both of these events take place within the context of the landing. In this sense it is not a cut from one scene to another which causes "magic" to occur but rather what Mathew Solomon describes as the horizontal strategy of "Méliès' reliance on substitution splices to create instantaneous and often imperceptible transitions or transformations *within* spaces."[31]

The second landing shows the capsule crashing into a small part of the moon's landscape, which does not seem to have any indications that it is part of an "eye."[32] This scene should be revelatory in the context of the astronomers gaining knowledge, since the surface of the moon has actually been reached: it is being stepped on, smelled and touched. However, the surface is theatrically fantastic, and not just according to standards imposed by those who have watched actual recordings of the lunar made by the Apollo 11 crew. This theatricality is an essential part of the film, as seen in the fact that the capsule lands more than once; for, as Gunning argues, "Clearly we are not supposed to think the ship actually landed twice."[33] Thus the dual landings have another purpose. If the first landing is about a fantastic experience of the moon, the second represents an effort to present a more proper lunar experience by differentiating what is found on the moon from the kinds of objects that are known on Earth. Thus the things found on the moon are bigger than those on Earth, or smaller, or a tree looks like a crystal, or a plant like a honeycomb. However, as in the first landing, verisimilitude is not the focus; it is rather the multiplicity and presencing of these different strategies of representation together. In other words, there is a tension created between both these strategies of vertical and horizontal gaps which then becomes a tension between the moon itself and its presentations on film. This is the essence of indirectness.

In other words, what is important in *Le Voyage* is that at the beginning of the history of the moon on film we can already see a multitude of strategies existing together on screen.[34] This is what Gunning calls the film's "collage-like space in which different modes of representation contend."[35] None of these representations are posited as potentially true (because their truth is negated by the others). Instead, this shifting indicates not only a multitude of perspectives, but also a multitude of possible modes of being for the object of the moon itself. As Harman argues, "Objects may change rapidly; they may be perceived differently by different observers; they remain opaque to all the efforts of knowledge to master them. But the very condition of all change, perspectivism, and opacity is that objects have a *definite character* that can change, be perceived, and resist."[36] In this sense the multitudinous moon in *Le Voyage* can be seen as a representation of the stable instability of objects themselves. This multiple core is then projected back on to the earth when it is seen from the lunar surface. In other words, techniques for representing the moon are seen as useful for representing the earth as well.

[Earthrise] These are big claims. Yet this is simply another way of saying that the moon's presence in our sky becomes a lens though which to see ourselves. This leads Scott Montgomery to claim that "The moon provides a purifying distance from which to view all of human sin, which, as Lucian teases, apparently composes the whole of human existence. *This* is the lunar secret, this distance that tears the mask off the close and familiar. The lunar disk becomes a lens focused on terrestrial realities, magnifying by miniaturizing, allowing a greater span of vision by physically reducing the earth to a region 'below.'"[37] This mirroring is seen in images of the earth shown from the surface of the moon. In *Le Voyage* this view is the first thing that takes place after the astronomers exit the capsule.

When the earth is seen the astronomers raise their arms, as if in praise. Then the scenery making up the flora of the moon lowers, as if on pulleys, leaving the earth in all of its glory alone, on center stage. This is a performance, meaning theater. Influenced by the pantomime theater of the time, here "Méliès was not offering an inadequate approximation of realism but a different style, based on acknowledged theatricality and illusion—a fairyland with a sense of humor and irony about itself."[38] There is no pretense at anything "natural" in this moonscape. It is part of Méliès' "magic." As André Gaudreault argues, "Méliès' elaborate sets are so stylized that there could be no doubt as to their patent artificiality."[39] At the same time, this performance is staged around a "real" object, Earth. In the Earthrise seen from the moon, Earth can be seen as depicted in a "realistic" fashion, meaning there is an attempt to escape the anthropomorphization involved in the moon man and other such fantastic presentations. This realistic earth in the midst of the moon-as-stage inserts a sense of verticality into the simultaneous presencing of different forms. This is what Murray Pomerance calls "the transitory image" in *Le Voyage,* meaning a double-figure which "merges two contradictory, two 'distant' states into a single moving—and thus emotional—experience."[40] One indication of the importance of seeing the earth from another celestial body for the film is signaled by the fact that the first thing the astronomers do after landing on the moon is to look up at their home planet. Immediately after this, they all lie down and immediately go to sleep, as if their work is done.

[Underground] The last aspect of *Le Voyage* to be discussed here also involves a doubling: because the moon is such a well-known figure of barrenness as seen from Earth's surface with the naked eye, in order to justify any kind of strangeness on it there is often a need to remove the moon one more step from human understanding, by going underground. The moon in this sense is *too* close and needs to be made even more distant. On the other hand, going underground has an unexpected effect: it actually makes the similarities of the moon and the earth *more* apparent. While on the surface the moon is made up of some kind of theatrically crystalline leaves, when the astronomers go underground they find a world very similar to the earth, only comically bigger and more malleable, involving giant flora.

Yet despite all of its difference, this underground zone of the moon in *Le Voyage* is much more like the earth than the lunar surface. Here are what can be called tree trunks, large mushrooms and honeycombs. This is not otherness but strangeness in the sense that what is familiar is taken and made strange rather than any attempt at constructing the new (and hence invisible and impossible).[41] This idea is supported by a later scene in which the capsule, on returning to Earth, plunges into the sea and then floats back up to the surface. This brief scene again takes place "under," although it is underwater rather than underground. Both offer similar exaggerations on familiar themes in order to create a sense of oddity. This comparison of the lunar underground with Earth's underwater world signals the role the underground moon scene has in the film: it is a place for objects of this world which are at the same time seen as estranged from this world. Thus in the underwater scene, "normal" jellyfish now take on a similarity to the giant mushrooms of the moon. In a sense, we are now seeing Earth from "below," but from on Earth itself.

In this underwater underground of the earth, the flat black silhouette of the capsule floats up against a matte painting of an underwater landscape. The jellyfish which are a part of our everyday lives (even if just from books) are brought into their "proper" strangeness by being read along with the oversized mushrooms of the moon. This is also the function of seeing the earth from the moon: what is normal becomes strange (when seen from another celestial body). Thus when, in the scene following the underwater one, the moon is once again seen from Earth's surface it is, just like the jellyfish, a familiar object now brought into an uncanny strangeness because. In other words, now both the earth and the moon are fuzzy.

This "strangeness" is what Harman means by "confrontation": it is a proper relation to an object which admits the violent strife between it and its sensual qualities.[42] This tension of the film's "aggressive visual style"[43] is brought about through the multitude of ways in which the moon is presented:

chalkboard fuzziness (a false understanding), fuzziness in the sky (the way the moon is actually seen from Earth), a face in the moon (fantasy) and strangeness on the surface (the unknown). However, there are actually more strategies than these four, which is a number privileged by Heidegger and Harman, for we also have the underground scene and the moon seen again from Earth's surface. Thus our reading of the moon shows that what is important about the fourfold is that it is a multitude. This idea of such a horizontal strategy of presentational variety will continue through many readings of various moons populating various films.

Chapter 2

Frau im Mond/Woman in the Moon (1929)

[Illustrations] The moon first appears in Fritz Lang's *Frau im Mond* in a number of illustrations pinned to the walls of Professor Mannfeldt's (Klaus Pohl) home. A number of years previously the Professor had a theory that gold could be found on the moon. He was a laughing stock then, although his ideas are now being reevaluated. The illustrations show that he has never given up on his idea.

Yet, the images have a different function than the moon and Earth on the blackboard of *Le Voyage*. In reading Méliès' film, a simple figuration was developed: the "emptiness" or "fuzziness" of the "telescopic moon" needed to be filled in by direct observation on the lunar surface. Nevertheless, the "inverted" gun used for launching the capsule was read as indicating a *loss* of vision since as the capsule approached the moon an increasingly fantastic moon was presented. Yet it was this fantastic moon which provided a path to lunar truth. In Lang's film a different set of coordinates are developed. The illustrations of the moon which line the walls of the Professor's apartment are clippings from various academic journals. The moon is in no way fuzzy, but rather an object of academic inquiry within a scientific community. Thus this moon has already been "filled in." This more "scientific" approach to the moon is reflected in the reception of the movie, which was called "a miracle becoming reality" upon its release; in addition, Albert Einstein was in the audience of its premiere and the film is credited for inventing the countdown.[44] This "scientific moon" is also indicated by the introduction of a new object: for, while the telescope has its place in the film's construction of lunar understanding, a globe of the moon is now also one of the results of lunar research, indicating that the moon has been understood from all sides, meaning in a kind of "entirety" which has no place in *Le Voyage*.

While in *Le Voyage* the "fuzzy" moon led to a tension between presentations of the moon and their object, in *Frau im Mond* tension is first seen in the figure of Professor Mannfeldt, who embodies both a scientific understanding of the moon and a very personal point of view about it at the same time. In a flashback near the beginning of the film he is shown being laughed off stage by his peers while giving a lecture on traveling to the moon to prospect for gold. Thus the images of the moon that plaster his walls and which are taken from scientific journals are not really about "accuracy," rather they indicate that there is a more personal element involved. This can be seen in how a long pan around the Professor's apartment, showing the various drawings and journals, stops on the only direct reference seen to the Professor in the scientific literature, a notice in the *Abendzeitung* that the Professor was laughed out of the scientific community for his ideas of a gold-filled moon. In addition, the Professor appears both in caricature and under what is presumably the journal title *Punch,* indicating his removal from the scientific community around him. Why he would hang these degrading pictures on his wall at home is uncertain, but it is clear that the scientific representations of the moon take on the role of showing how the Professor is actually at odds with the scientific community. In this sense there is a "personal" element added to the objective scientific observations of the moon: the Professor's point of view.[45]

Thus rather than developing a number of different presentational strategies regarding putting the moon on film (seen on the blackboard, the approach and the lunar surface in *Le Voyage,* for example), Lang's film presents a distance between the observer and the observed, seen here as a gap between the Professor's "personal" obsession with the moon and the scientific understanding of it seen in the academic journals. This difference does not indicate a need for the observer to "adjust" in order to "see" correctly but rather it indicates that the distance between an object and its observers forms another version of Harman's "indirectness," which played a role in the last chapter.

[Rocket Vision] The gap between observer and object is further heightened in the next images of the moon in the film, which have been taken by an unmanned rocket, the H32, which was sent to photograph the moon from orbit. Although humans made the rocket and its cameras, here, for the first time that I have found in the history of "moon films," images of the moon are shown which have been taken without a human sitting behind the viewfinder. Thus, as Marie Lathers argues, the technical necessities for recording the moon come into focus: "*Woman in the Moon* is... a film that projects the project of making a film about the moon."[46] The cameras of the rocket are described and shown in detail, leading to Tom Gunning's comment that in lieu of human drama the film focuses on "the pure spectacle of technology."[47] The rocket cameras are connected to a timer which activates the shutter. In addition, there are three different lenses attached to the camera in the nose of the rocket, looking more like the multiple-imaging mechanism of an insect than the kind of camera a human could operate. What this rocket-camera perspective results in are images which go beyond human experience, capturing an aspect of the moon which no human had ever seen: the dark side. Because its rotational period is the same time as the period of its orbit, the far side of the moon perpetually remains on the opposite side of Earth. A photograph of the unseen side is thus one of reasons for launching the H32.

These far-side images immediately suggest a sense of speculation lacking in images of the near-side: the side of the moon that can be seen from Earth is known to be free of alien "Selenites," but what about the other? Once again the part of the moon that is visible from Earth is too familiar; what is needed is another level of removal from Earth-vision for fantasy to take place. *Le Voyage*, along with other films such as *Cat-Women of the Moon* (1953), uses the trope of the underground to state this level of fantasy; here it takes place on the dark side. And although no life is found on the dark side in *Frau im Mond*, Lang used its unknownness as an excuse to show the astronauts on the surface breathing air normally (they land on the dark side), for at the time of filming it was known that the moon was without atmosphere.[48] However, this image of the dark side does more than engender speculation, it foregrounds a gap between the observer and the object. This is because the dark side is connected to that which cannot be seen by human observation. In this sense it has much to do with the thought of Quentin Meillassoux regarding the independence of objects from human observation.

[Ancestrality] In the first chapter, a gap was developed between the multiple presentations of the moon in *Le Voyage* and the moon itself. The visibility of this gap arose out of the differences between a sensual object and its sensual qualities. These differences came out of two main events: the differences of the presentations from each other and the obvious theatricality of the presentations. However, the "gap" created by these differences was left largely unexamined. Although containing some fundamental differences from Harman's position (developed below), Meillassoux's concept of *ancestrality* will begin to define this gap and to set the stage for some of the major problems in coming to an understanding of the gap between one object and another.

In brief, while the earth is 4.5 billion years old, humanity, in the form of *Homo habilis*, has only been around for about 2 million years. For Meillassoux, "contemporary science is in a position to precisely determine—albeit in the form of revisable hypotheses—the dates of the formation of the fossils of creatures living prior to the emergence of the first hominids, the date of the accretion of the earth, the date of the formation of stars, and even the 'age' of the universe itself."[49] Meillassoux uses these facts to develop how this gap between object (the earth) and observer (all of humanity) can be known. To do this, Meillassoux attacks two possible objections to the problem of ancestrality. First, it could be argued that yes, the earth is 4.56 billion years old, but then add, *for the scientist*. This is the "codicil of modernity"[50] which argues that even if no one were there to observe the formation of the earth, we talk about it *as if* someone were there. What is problematic about this supposition is that it includes science within thought, while science actually determines the *emergence* of thought, and thus thought lies *within* science.[51] This is because the earth existed before humans, and thus humans exist within the world, rather than the world within human thought.

Yet it could be also be argued that confusion is taking place between the empirical question of how the body of the earth came to be and the transcendental question of how science can come to know such facts.[52] Meillassoux answers this objection thus: in order for the world to be filtered through thought (i.e., the transcendentalist position) thought must take place; for thought to take place it is connected to a point of view (i.e., subjectivity); for a point of view to take place it must be located in a body; this means that bodies must exist in order for a point of view to exist; the earth existed before human bodies existed, thus the transcendental point of view is historically contingent (it arose, at the earliest, with the first human bodies); in other words, since something exists outside bodies (pre-human earth) something exists outside thought (the earth before thought was on it, for example).[53]

In *Frau im Mond* this relationship between objects and thought came forth in how rocket H32 recorded the dark side of the moon "on its own," meaning without a human behind the lens pushing a button. However, it is only the approach to the moon and landing on its surface which begin to bring forth some of the complexities of this line of thought.

[Sunrise] In other words, during the approach to the moon the rocket has a similar function as the distance of cinema, for as Laurence Rickels argues in a reading of the novel on which *Frau im Mond* was based (written by Lang's wife, Thea von Harbou), "On the way to the moon, the spaceship serves as a lookout post for a motion picture camera…."[54] This can be seen in the first view from the camera/rocket that is shown after take-off: the sun is seen "rising" over the edge of the earth. This image of the earth is different from that shown in *Le Voyage*. The discussion of the earthrise in Méliès' film highlighted the way that seeing the earth from off the earth brought about a sense of estrangement which made the connections or relations between objects more palpable. However, in Lang's film the first image of Earth from afar is quite different. This is not just because the earth is seen from the window of the rocket rather than from the surface of the moon, but rather because a different set of relations is involved: the sun is actually seen "rising" from behind the earth. This difference causes two things to happen: 1) this scene of strangeness is automatically more familiar by being connected to the daily rising of the sun; 2) thus it is not the "thing" which is strange or which changes, nor its difference from presentational strategies (a horizontal strategy of a multitude of simultaneous representations seen in *Le Voyage*), but rather the relation of one object and another. In other words, what is seen is that the sun never really "rises" at all; it merely seems so because the movement of the earth in relation to the sun creates the appearance of sunrises and sunsets.

This reading of the scene brings forth the manner in which a sense of space, or the location of the observer, is constructed. Gunning's discussion of *Frau im Mond* in *The Films of Fritz Lang* also focuses on the role of space in the film. First Gunning claims that Lang's film is devoid of characterization, being more of a film about (as quoted above) "the pure spectacle of technology."[55] Then he introduces his discussion on space by quoting a comment Jacques Rivette made on the film: "'the plot primarily served Lang as a pretext for his first attempt at a *totally closed* world.'"[56] Gunning uses this quote to develop a two-fold thesis about how in *Frau im Mond* the characters' experience of space conflates an "agoraphobic fear of infinite extension with a claustrophobic fear of entrapment."[57] The first "fold" of the thesis is illustrated by the expansiveness of space and the emptiness of the moon, while the second is illustrated by the confining space of the interior of the rocket. At first this seems a perfect illustration of the argument regarding the position of the observers while seeing the sun and Earth: seeing the movement of both celestial bodies emphasizes the expansiveness of space while the passengers trapped in the rocket traveling through space emphasize the confinements of the ship. However, if we go back to Rivette's quote and provide some context for his idea of a totally closed world, a different reading of this scene develops.

The quote from Rivette appears in his essay "The Hand," which is not a review of *Frau im Mond* but of Lang's last American film, *Beyond a Reasonable Doubt* (1956). The latter film tells the story of a man who sets out to question the validity of circumstantial evidence by planting clues to a fake murder to see if someone can be wrongfully prosecuted, although of course a real murder is uncovered in the process. What strikes Rivette in his review is the lifelessness of the film: he says that it plays more like a script-reading than acting and that there is no justification for the actions presented, rather there is just a "world of necessity,"[58] prompting him to ask "what part of life, even inhuman, can subsist in a quasi-abstract universe which is nevertheless within the range of possible universes?"[59] It is at this point that Rivette makes his comment, which Gunning quotes, about *Frau im Mond* being the first attempt at such a being-less world.[60] However, this closer look at Rivette's essay indicates that it is actually the object-ness of the space in *Frau im Mond* which catches Rivette's attention; in other words, the way that the space exists *outside* of the "life" of the human observer.

The way in which this "outside" is achieved in Lang's film is not through negating the observer by canceling her out but rather by foregrounding such a position; in other words, to connect this with Meillassoux's thought discussed above, Lang stresses the presence of the *body* in which a point of view is located, thus showing that if a body can be *there* on the earth seeing a sunrise, or *here* in a rocket seeing the earth move in relation to the sun, then this "sunrise" exists in relation to many bodies with many locations of points of view, thus indicating that the sunrise could exist no matter where a body were located, even if it were located *nowhere*. In this sense, as Raymond Bellour argues regarding Lang's work, "The subject is often a vagrant body, only one object among other objects."[61]

This foregrounding of the location of the observer can also be seen in two shots of the rocket crew as they are watching the sun appear from behind the earth: first they are shown in the window of the rocket in darkness, observing the earth before the sun appears from behind it; shortly after this they are seen in the light of the sun which has just "risen."

The variability of the physical location of the scientists on the rocket (changing from dark to illuminated) is foregrounded along with the movement of the earth in relation to the sun. While in *Le Voyage* the presentations of the moon were in conflict, here it is the changing positions of the viewers and objects which are highlighted. The physicality of the embodied point of view is again shown when Friede (Gerda Maurus) and the boy Gustav (Gustl Gstettenbaur) are seen at the window, using their hands to block out the earth through forced perspective. In this sense *Frau im Mond* is typically Langian in the manner in which the position of the viewer is constructed. As Bellour argues, for Lang "There is one strictly univocal manner of framing a character's vision: to enclose the shot of the seen object between two identical shots of the seeing subject. Lang seldom does more than indicate the possibility of such certitude, and then only to challenge it immediately and to plunge it into an equivocality."[62] This equivocality indicates that subjects have no privileged status in relation to objects: both are equally unstable because it is the relations between them which are becoming more visible.

[Approach] This foregrounding of the instability (meaning unsanctioned, or ungiven) of the spatial relationship between the observer and the object becomes clearer during the approach of the rocket to the moon. The first time the moon is seen during this part of the film is through one of the "portholes" of the rocket. The moon traverses the window from left to right, eventually filling the window perfectly. The reason that this shot foregrounds the role of the viewer is simply that the point of view is specified: the way that the moon fits "perfectly" into the frame created by the circular porthole of the rocket stresses both the sight of the moon itself and the vehicle through which it is being seen; thus it is not only the fact that the moon is being seen close-up that is important, but that it is being seen by humans in a rocket ship. This is an example of Meillassoux's argument that a point of view located in a body shows that the universe encompasses bodies (and thus thought) rather than the other way around. The fact that it is the moon which is being seen is also important for this scene, for just as the earth existed before humankind, so has the moon, which is considered to be only slightly younger than the earth. In other words, this location from which the moon is seen from the rocket represents the gap between the point of view and the object viewed. As Bellour argues, "It is by means of the fissures—by means of the gaps which [Lang] sets up—that he can be understood."[63]

Yet this is not the only example of a foregrounded point of view in relation to the rocket and the moon. When the rocket approaches the dark side of the moon where it will land, the earth is seen to set behind the moon in a similar manner, with the location of the observers being highlighted in a manner similar to when the earth is seen sinking behind a quickly spinning lunar surface. The reason that this simplistic notion of point-of-view and subject-object relations is being put forth here is just to begin illustrating the manner in which fixing a point of view to a location allows for something to take place at a different location.

[Landing] Upon landing, however, another element is introduced: the moon, seen out of the rocket window, speeds by at such a quick pace that it becomes blurred. With this image, instead of the location of the bodies which house a mobile point of view being foregrounded it is objects themselves which begin to spin out of control. One result of this "accelerated" moon seen on descent is that the locality of the observers is foregrounded through their contrast with the rapid spinning of the moon.

In one sense this change in speed of the moon is just meant to represent the rapid descent of the rocket to the lunar surface. However, it also indicates that the object itself is weirder than has been let on. This weirdness is also reflected in how upon approaching the lunar surface the scientific understanding previously displayed about the moon disintegrates. Once again, the closer the astronauts get, the stranger the moon appears. In other words, the accelerated surface is expressive, while the previous scientifically understood one is static. This is an important difference as the rocket approaches the surface, and it is reflected in Professor Mannfeldt's reaction to the landing: he both wants to turn the ship around at all costs and he fights to keep all of the viewing hatches open when the rest of the crew attempts to close them, as if he has become drugged on the disturbing speed of the moon.

The Professor's reactions are justified: he has lost the scientific moon for which he gave up his reputation. Now, face to face with the accelerated pace of the expressive moon, he loses all sense of reality. He is as mad as the scientific journals have painted him.

In this scene two different elements are brought together: the location of points of view in space in the bodies which are located and the separation of the object from it presentations, seen in the accelerated moon differing from the scientific and static presentations of it seen so far.[64]

[Acceleration] The term *accelerated* is being used here in an aesthetic sense as a "revved-up deployment of forms."[65] Another word for this movement is *cinema*. In *Philosophy and the Moving Image* John Mullarkey argues that the manner in which cinema itself philosophizes is that at times movement can engage thought. However, in cinema the role of movement is perhaps better approached through a reading of time since it is when images are faster or slower than their surrounding context that attention is called to them and thought engaged: "Certain things make us think, and those things, so this argument goes, are ultimately types of time. Things happen on screen that give us pause for thought, but what must happen first is that film pauses itself—its normal speeds—to make us think at all that something out of the ordinary is happening."[66] Gestures in cinema can take "too long," like a sugar cube slowly dissolving in a scene from Krzysztof Kieslowski's *Three Colors: Blue* (1993).[67] Mullarkey argues that this estrangement of a gesture reclaims the gesture from being lost in the bustle of the everyday. Here Mullarkey quotes Benjamin Noys who is generally credited with foregrounding the term *acceleration* in philosophical discourse by arguing that change can come about by speeding up the rules of a system rather than attacking a system from the outside: "if capitalism generates its own forces of dissolution then the necessity is to radicalize capitalism itself: the worse the better. We can call this tendency accelerationism."[68] While Noys himself has been one of the first to cast doubts on the political validity of accelerationism, much work has been done to co-opt it as an aesthetic concept, led by Steven Shaviro's call for an accelerationist aesthetics at the end of his *Post Cinematic Affect*.[69] This is an essentially different kind of accelerationism than Mullarkey's in that rather than engendering thought it encourages destruction.

But is one of these accelerations true for *Frau im Mond*? The thinking acceleration of Mullarkey or the destructive acceleration of Noys, and are these so mutually exclusive? The accelerated moon seen in the landing is disturbing because it makes the position of the observers visible: their location in the rocket ship is foregrounded by the view of the rapidly rotating moon. This would seem to fit into the ability of speed in cinema to reclaim a gesture forgotten in the speed of everyday events. However, another shot from the moon landing seems to function differently. As the rocket passes along the moon surface before touching down it is almost indistinguishable from the shadowy craters of the lunar surface. In this shot the speed of the rocket, briefly, nearly matches the speed of the moon. Here the reflection of the sun's light off the rocket makes it look similar to that of the craters on the moon. The rocket seems to be part of the moon itself. This actually seems to fit into Noys' reading of acceleration as destruction: the rocket-as-subject is lost in the moon-as-object. This is because the speed of the rocket matches that of the moon, it catches up to it, fulfills it, and is thus rendered nearly invisible, or nearly destroyed. Yet it raises another issue: the rocket and moon seem to be in relation to each other. In this sense acceleration is similar to the way that the relation between objects is manifest in the discussion of point of view above.

[Surface] The first element of acceleration is about making an everyday event or gesture visible, such as showing the falseness of every sun "rise." The second element is about utilizing the coordinates of a system in order to disrupt a system—this was seen in the way that the accelerated moon subsumed the rocket during landing. This foregrounds, if nothing else, how the rocket and moon are in relation to each other. This "in relation to each other" was also seen in the gathering of the fourfold in the discussion of Heidegger's *das Geviert* in the previous chapter. The first images seen in the film from a point of view on the surface of the moon contain such a gathering of difference together, which we could also call the time of change. Once the film moves to the lunar surface there is a gathering of emptiness (the "scientific" perspective) and fantasy. When the rocket lands on the moon it sends up a cloud of dust, and when a rope ladder is lowered from the entryway it unfurls on sand, signaling that this moon is realistic in the sense of not being made of green cheese. However, the "reality" of the sand stands in contrast to the fantastic mountain ranges surrounding the landing site. Yet, what makes the image of the rocket landing interesting is that it indicates what has been used to gather the two elements of acceleration together: the rocket ship. The rocket ship stands in the middle of both the real sandy surface and the fantastic mountain ranges, in a position of fusion, as a locus of change. In other words, the rocket stands for the mechanism of the gap in a horizontal tension between the sandy surface and rocky surroundings.

The rocket is also what allows for the always-physical location of point of view in a body to become visible in the film. The astronauts were removed from their home world, first into space and then onto the moon; this is what Benedict Singleton calls "a jailbreak at the maximum possible scale."[70] Another way to look at it is through the connection between the rocket and the role of localization: to see the same object from another point of view foregrounds the location of the point of view—this location takes place in a body (here, the rocket). Following Meillassoux, this body can then be posited to begin its existence *after* the beginning of the existence of the earth, and thus the connection with time comes forth. This aspect was not brought out in *Le Voyage,* where different presentational strategies "merely" developed a gap between an object and its qualities. In Lang's film the localized nature of a point of view is developed.

[Camera] Upon landing on the moon the scientists split into two factions: Professor Mannfeldt and the American Turner (Fritz Rasp) are convinced there is gold to be found so they go off to explore the surface, an adventure which eventually ends in their deaths. Back at the rocket, Helius (Willy Fritsch) stays behind trying to fix the ship in order to get home. At the same time, the only female astronaut—Freide (Gerda Maurus)—makes some observations of the surface. As a part of this research, Freide takes a movie camera and tripod to record some moving images of the landscape. In the scene with the movie camera Freide is shown changing a role of film, setting the camera running, and then leaving it (perhaps once again) to film the surface of the moon alone, with no one behind the viewfinder.

Thus a different object than that of the rocket ship is situated in the middle of both a scientific and a fantastic moon. The rocket ship gathered change around itself because it offered a point of view that could be localized in a body and thus seen as separate from an object. But how does an unwomanned camera fit into this equation? In one sense the camera differs from the rocket because it is a movie camera being used in a movie, thus it could be argued that the camera is more than a camera, it is the metaphor for cinema. Mullarkey argues that the thought or philosophy of cinema resides in time: its slowing down or speeding up led to thought about why this was happening. Yet the camera here is an image of recording time without humanity, for there is no one standing behind it as it films. In this sense the camera has a similar function to that of the moon—both indicate the other-than-human, or what has been called ancestrality.[72] The way that the camera in *Frau im Mond* can move beyond or outside the human was seen earlier in the film when the unmanned H32 rocket made the dark side of the moon visible for the first time.[73] Here, the unwomanned camera presents an access to that which exists without human thought, the camera recording alone in space.[74]

The rest of the film offers little in the way of different representations of the moon. There is a short underground scene, but it is more a scene of adventure than difference. Then at the end of the film Helius stays on the planet, seemingly alone, having tricked Friede and the others to return home on the rocket without him (there is only enough oxygen for some of the astronauts to return). However, at the end of the film Freide sneaks off the rocket and decides to spend her remaining days with Helius on the surface. The desolateness of the moon is shown when Helius is seen alone, thinking his love has taken off forever, while perhaps the fantasy of the moon is seen in the way the camera remains on the embrace of the reunited lovers at the end of the film, suggesting that their love will be enough to survive even the most terrible of fates. This gathering of the reality of desolation and the elation of fantasy is a repetition of what happened in the scenes with the rocket and the lonely camera, both of which foregrounded the role of gathering in relation to point of view.[75]

Chapter 3

Kosmicheskiy Reys/The Cosmic Voyage (1936)

[Pre-Launch] In distinction to the two previous films examined, in Vasili Zhuravlov's *Kosmicheskiy Reys/The Cosmic Voyage*, made for Mosfilm in 1936, there is a total absence of lunar images in the scenes before the cosmonauts approach the moon; some other lunar tropes do appear, however. For example, two telescopes for lunar observations are seen: a small one in the home of lead scientist Pavel Ivanovich Sedikh (Sergei Komarov) and a large-scale telescope in Sedikh's laboratory. However, what is seen through these telescopes is not shown during this part of the film. When such a telescopic view does take place, it is later, in relation to the rocket passengers seeing the moon from their ship; in other words, the only time the moon is seen from the earth is when it is in dialogue with the moon seen from space.

In addition, at the beginning of the film the moon is absent from numerous nocturnal shots of the skyline of a futuristic Moscow (the film was made in 1936 and features a Moscow from 1947). Yet there is "space" for it, as can be seen in a shot which features a completed version of the planned (and never finished) Palace of the Soviets building, with a "missing" moon which could easily appear in the upper right-hand corner.[76] Thus it might be argued that there is a *resistance* to representing the moon before the space travelers make visual contact with it. There are plenty of opportunities to do so,[77] as seen in another chance for the moon to make an appearance, during the scene in Professor Sedikh's home when he is arguing with his wife about what to pack for the space voyage. A globe is shown on a desk, calling to mind the lunar sphere of *Frau im Mond*. However, this is neither a lunar nor a terrestrial globe, but an astronomical one, meaning it is a black sphere with white dots representing stars and other celestial bodies.

These are all possible moments in which the moon could appear in the first part of the film. What this resistance indicates will only be answered when such presentations actually begin to take place. What can be hazarded at this point is that presenting the moon is not of the utmost importance for this film, otherwise it would have happened already. Instead the focus will lie elsewhere. I argue that instead of concentrating on *presenting* the moon *The Cosmic Voyage* attempts to show an *experience* of it.

[The Approach] A resistance to presenting also takes place during the approach to the moon. "Let's open the portholes and start observing" cries Professor Sedikh, and the cosmonauts open the large portholes only to be confronted with a clear field of stars and "nothing" else, meaning no Earth and no Moon. In this sense direct observation does not work: if you open the window and just look out you will see nothing. This is important because when the moon finally does make an appearance it is through a different kind of window, a fuzzy one; this view also takes place via a different kind of mechanism, a dissolve.

Professor Sedikh is manning the main control console and directing the rest of the crew on how to look for the moon. However, it is he who finds it. "His" porthole is different from the others. It is made of a kind of grid, or mesh, through which the moon begins to appear only faintly in a dissolve. As the rocket nears the moon the dissolve continues although it never "completes"; something always lies between the moon and the screen. This "something" is at first the grid of the window, although this is eventually replaced by a kind of fog, or steam of humidity, which stands between Sedikh and the moon.

Nothing disturbed the view between the subject and the stars in the first views out of the portholes, although the moon was not visible either. Thus there is either something about seeing the moon itself that causes such disruption or there is a need for such disruption in order to see the moon. At the same time, the appearance of the moon causes something else to happen in the film. As soon as the moon is sighted from the rocket ship the story of the film returns to Earth. Lunar images are then presented as seen from the point of view of scientists observing the moon through terrestrial telescopes; the lunar images that were absent before the rocket launch are now taking place.

There are three types of Earth-based lunar image now shown in the film: the whole moon located in space in its first-quarter phase, with a high contrast between dark and light sections; a closer shot of the surface of the moon with realistic craters shown; and finally an "accelerated" moon appears when the scientists scan the surface for a sign that the rocket has landed. These three "types" of observations of the scientists on Earth have been discussed up to this point. The high-contrast moon is similar to Méliès' fuzzy moon waiting to be filled by the observations of humans who will land on its surface: the whiteness of the light side and the complete blackness of the dark side attest to this. A second type of presentation is seen in how the close-up of the moon actually only shows only a "quarter" of its light side. In this sense it reflects the more scientific moon seen in the beginning of *Frau im Mond*, especially in the images brought back by the unmanned rocket. However, in order for this section of the moon to be shown scientifically it needs to be shown partially: there is no attempt at seeing the moon as a "whole," as was seen with the moon-globe in Lang's film.[78] The last image of the moon is accelerated, representing what the terrestrial scientists see as they scan its surface. This acceleration is similar to Noys' in which speed disrupts an object; however, in *The Cosmic Voyage* movement takes place on the earth due to the rapid movement of a scanning telescope (although it is difficult to imagine such fluid dexterity for the massive telescope shown), rather than being caused by the descent of the rocket itself. Thus it is not just the location of those on the rocket which is being foregrounded but the mode of observation of those on the earth. So once strange things happen in the proximity of the moon, strange things start happening on Earth too.

When we next see the moon from the rocket it is just before it lands. The moon is seen once again through Professor Sedikh's porthole, and at first it seems like a similar scene to that in *Frau im Mond* when the moon was viewed through the rocket window, fitting perfectly inside. However, there are two differences in *The Cosmic Voyage*: the medium of the porthole is still visible in the form of a semi-transparent mesh, although it looks different than when the moon was first seen through it, and the approaching moon does not only fit into the frame of the porthole but supersedes it, spilling beyond the upper side of its frame. This approach to the moon in *The Cosmic Voyage* highlights a number of presentational strategies: the medium through which the moon is seen is foregrounded, images of the moon seen from the rocket are cut with images of the moon seen at the same time from Earth, and finally, and most importantly, the image of the moon is seen to first fit in and then supersede the frame through which it is observed. This last strategy, that of superseding is not a "new" aspect of the moon confined to its appearance in film but rather an illustration of its actual process of formation-by-accretion, as Jane Grant argues (while quoting Italo Calvino's story "The Mushroom Moon"): "In escaping the confinement of its own internal structure, matter *exceeds* its materiality, transgresses its form and structure. It is potent, an action and no longer just a substance. Here matter is in the process of becoming, a concentration of forming and reforming 'passages of immensities' that overspill the static."[79] This exceeding informs another way of reading how the moon is located in a space in which it escapes knowledge, as seen in the thought of Harman and Meillassoux.

[Speculative Moon] There are two points in Graham Harman's

Quentin Meillassoux: Philosophy in the Making in which he addresses the moon explicitly. The first time is to make his standard criticism of Meillassoux which boils down to ancestrality not being enough. Harman says that "continuing to exist following the death of humans is only *one* aspect of the independence of things from us. The other aspect is that they must be independent of us *right now*."[80] This point is important for Harman because he believes that Meillassoux's thought does not have "the proper degree of depth" because synchronous things can also feature a "withdrawal behind its accessibility to thought."[81] What this inaccessibility entails was outlined in the first chapter: a set of relations between elements which remains unknown, or in other words, "a unifying principle never exhausted by all attempts to approach it from the outside."[82] It is easy to see how the moon fits into this argument for Harman, because "to challenge the thought-world correlate we need not ask about the ancestral moon before any thinking creatures arose. For even the 'synchronic' moon in the moment you read this sentence continues to orbit and sleep and attract in a way that our knowledge of the moon cannot fathom and certainly cannot replace."[83] This inaccessibility has been seen in this study in the manner in which the moon becomes more fantastic the closer it becomes, although the next argumentative step would be to see the inaccessibility of relations within this fantastic element itself. This is the thesis of the next section of the book, on camp films.

Meillassoux also uses the moon and it appears in his discussion of why he privileges time over space when writing about objects existing outside thought. In *After Finitude* he first defines Harman's criticism through an imaginary interlocutor who states that "craters on the moon are actually 'closer' to us, from the viewpoint of the argument under consideration, than a vase falling in a country house when there is nobody there. The observed craters, in effect, pose no problem whatsoever to correlationism [Meillassoux's term for the viewpoint that all understanding is encapsulated by human thought], since they are connected to a subject who apprehends them, whereas according to you the fallen vase would pose such a problem, since it went un-witnessed."[84] Thus the interlocutor of Meillassoux's book assumes one aspect of Harman's position, which is that a difference in space is the same as a difference in time. For Meillassoux, who added this portion on distance to the English translation of *After Finitude*,[85] ancestrality is different because it posits an object which exists *before* all possibility of thought, and "Therein lies its singularity and its critical potency with regard to correlationism," or the belief in a "relative" or idealistic universe in which nothing can be known outside human thought.[86]

Thus in one sense Harman's critique is "softened" by the way Meillassoux indicates that ancestrality is only a *privileged* critical tool rather than an idiosyncratic philosophical position. However, as seen from the preceding discussion of early lunar films, the moon can function as a more complex metaphor than just something which can be seen from a distance. This complexity is brought out through the different presentational strategies used when it is put on film. These strategies include: using multiple presentational techniques in the same film (Méliès) which causes a gap to open between the object and its presentations; concretizing the location of the observer (Lang) which causes a gap to open between the observer and the presentations; and what is being developed in this chapter (Zhuravlov) under the aegis of an *experience* of the moon which seems to challenge the hegemony of its actual presentation. While these strategies will be dissected and expanded in the following chapters, at this point it can be seen that this discussion of shooting the moon defines the moon as a privileged object of interest in terms of something which lies "beyond." In this sense something which is far away but which can be seen puts the moon in a different position than either Meillassoux or Harman allows for it.[87]

[Surface] Part of the importance of the metaphor of the moon lies in the resistance to presentation found in *The Cosmic Voyage*. Upon landing on the surface Professor Sedikh again looks out of the rocket porthole. The surface is seen for the first time by a human standing upon it, thus indicating that the "distance" under discussion has been conquered. At the same time this vision is not so clear, for although the porthole is not the "main" one which was used for the dissolve discussed above, the residue of the medium through which the moon is being seen is even more pronounced, meaning that the lunar surface is barely visible due to the smudgy window. Landing on the surface thus results in almost zero visibility. The window is streaked with dirt and the effect of this hindrance is multiplied by the bright light from outside. The source of this light is not given. It is either the sun or the reflection of the sun off the moon. In a sense it does not matter which, for what is important is that the moon is not seen, rather than the mechanism of its invisibility.

At the same time, the stage for the role of experience (rather than presentation) in the film is set before the rocket even lands on the planet. A brief shot shows the rocket passing over the surface of the moon before landing. This is the first time that the moon is shown in close-up without the aid of a telescope. What is interesting about this scene is that the surface of the planet over which the rocket passes is different from any surface seen so far in lunar films. Instead of a sandy plain surrounded by a rocky mountain range which is never explored, the moon is shown as consisting of a rocky surface throughout, with most of the screen space being devoted to the mountainous nether-regions which will be the setting for most of the moon-action of the film.

The reason that these mountains are seen as setting up a reading of experience is that when the cosmonauts do exit the ship nearly the first thing they do is take off their weighted shoes and go "jump around" the mountainous region, experiencing the effects of the lower gravity of the moon. The mountains seem to be set up for this kind of experience, for wherever the cosmonauts go there are a series of steps or plateaus to bounce up and down upon (Figure 1).

Figure 1. *Kosmicheskiy Reys/The Cosmic Voyage* (1935).
With permission from Mosfilm.

There is almost no chance to walk in a straight line on the moon. The techniques for representing this mobility include the actors being strung on sometimes-visible wires and stop-motion animation. Whatever the technique, it is not the strangeness of how the moon looks which is important but rather how it influences action. This de-emphasizing of lunar presentation was also seen in the "blurry" windows of the rocket ship, which did not clear up upon landing.

[Lunar map] Another resistance to presenting the moon is seen in a new element in these films, which is the use of a lunar map. After the initial hopping around, one of the cosmonauts stops on one of the plateaus and unfolds a small map. With this scene an interesting relationship to where the cosmonauts are develops. They enjoy being on the moon, shown by their bouncing over the surface, but they have not really looked around (just as is seen, for example, in *Destination Moon* (1950), discussed below). Their use of the map shows something quite simple, that they have no idea where they are. They have landed on the dark side of the moon, of which they have no representations (for unlike the unmanned rocket sent in Lang's film, previous missions in Zhurlavlov's film have only tested whether a living creature can survive spaceflight: there have not been any photographic missions). The problem is that the landscape does not match their map, a fact which is buffeted by the next shot in which a cosmonaut looks up into the sky, expecting to see the earth, but is faced with an empty canvas of stars. In this sense the lunar map fulfills the function of all pre-space age lunar maps, which was, according to Bernd Brunner, that "unlike maps of Earth, visual representations of the moon didn't help travelers orient themselves in little-known terrain. Their function was largely symbolic—even though the moon was out of physical reach, mapping it had an imaginative value."[88] The "imaginative value" of the map in *The Cosmic Voyage* remains in how the astronauts find themselves "off the map" meaning that they need to struggle to get back on it in order to find a location from which to signal home that they have arrived. The use of the map on the moon also helps illustrate the role of experience in the film. While in *Le Voyage* looking at the earth from the moon was the first thing the astronomers did upon landing, and in *Frau im Mond* the earth was seen even before landing, here it is *bouncing* which takes precedence, and then an artistic representation of the moon (the map) is looked at before the earth is searched for in the sky, although even then it is not found. This indicates that rather than focusing on representing the moon, the film privileges an experience of the way being on the moon as different from being on Earth.

[Experience] James Attlee's book on the moon and its light, *Nocturne: A Journey in Search of Moonlight*, locates experience at the heart of the role the moon plays in our lives. After lamenting various ways in which our illuminated world blocks out the night sky, Attlee, on a walk in the countryside in Wales, states that "To experience moonlight at this intensity in a semi-urban setting in the twenty-first century feels like a privilege. At the same time, it can only hint at what a moonlit night would have been like before the arrival of humankind in the furthest corners of the earth."[89] In the context of the arguments being developed here, what jumps out from this quote is a connection between the moon and a time before humans. In addition, access to this "before" takes place through a "hint," an *indirect* communication; there is something about the moon that resists directness. Attlee suggests this in two seemingly contradictory statements made on the same page. First he asks "What is the source of our deep and enduring fascination with the moon, that has placed it at the centre of our consciousness since prehistoric times and that still works on the human mind today? Perhaps the answer is beyond words, something that must be lived." Thus a similar argument to that read into *The Cosmic Voyage* is taking shape regarding experience: presentations of the moon do not do it justice, instead one must experience it, as the cosmonauts do by jumping around on its relatively low-gravity surface. However, Attlee then suggests that "Such experiences are accessible today for most of us only through the words of a poet like Tu Fu, writing in China in the eighth century AD"; thus an experience which is "beyond words" actually lies within words, but the estranged words of poetry.

This "doubling" of the moon in Attlee is similar to the way in which in *The Cosmic Voyage* the moon is only seen from the earth *after* the cosmonauts have made visual contact with it through the vehicle of their rocket. This dialogue developed between the "blurry" moon seen through the technique of a dissolve from the rocket window can be seen as similar to Attlee's "beyond words," what was previously called a "vertical tension," while the more scientific moon seen via telescope from Earth can be connected to the "words" of the poetry of Tu Fu, a "horizontal tension." The fact that both these modes are seen in the same sequence in the film, and on the same page in Attlee, indicates that there is something to be said about their being present together. My argument is that this "something" denotes experience.

A key figure in a discussion of experience, especially as it relates to cinema, is Walter Benjamin. Attlee discusses Benjamin's essay "The Moon," in which he quotes Benjamin's discussion of the disruptive power of the moon (which Benjamin experiences upon waking up in his room): "'The first thing my glance encountered were the two cream-colored bowls of the washing utensils. During the day it never occurred to me to find fault with them but in the moonlight the blue band that ran around the upper part of the tumblers disturbed me. It looked deceivingly like a piece of material that was worming its way in and out of a seam.'"[90] Moonlight disturbs representation, it makes everyday things in their everyday light difficult to see. Recognizing this difficulty, to put it briefly, is what Benjamin calls experience. It could also be called poetry. Attlee indicates this linguistic tension when he calls attention to the doubled structure of experience for Benjamin: "As the writer that he will become, he has no choice but to recognize the existence of something that is dedicated to eradicating existence itself."[91] The openness to the eradication of representation is what is being called "experience" here. For Benjamin, a privileged place for this experience is the cinema.

In "One-Way Street," Benjamin, in a discussion of the decreased distance of new forms of media, advertising and the cinema, says that "In the cinema people whom nothing moves or touches any longer learn to cry again."[92] What is important here is the ability of cinema to move, or disturb a viewer stuck in the everyday into experiencing emotion again. In "Benjamin and

Cinema" Miriam Bratu Hansen argues that for Benjamin such interruptions take on a doubled structure because the *possibility* of interruption "would make the protective shield against stimuli, the precarious boundary or rind of the bodily ego, a bit less of a carapace or armor and a bit more of a matrix or medium—a porous interface between the organism and the world that would allow for a greater mobility and circulation of psychic energies."[93] This porous mobility can be seen as the "doubling" of the rocket-moon and telescope-moon in *The Cosmic Voyage* and as the "wordless" and "poetic" moon in Attlee. As Hansen argues, cinema is one location for the potentiality of such doubling: "film has the potential to reverse, in the form of *play*, the catastrophic consequences of an *already failed* reception of technology."[94] This idea of "play" was seen in the first chapter in the form of multiple representations of the moon in the same film, and in the second with the variable locality of the observer which then caused a distance from and between presentations to become visible. In the next part of this book this play will come under the rubric of the ways in which the moon *remains* present in the wild and varied fantasies of camp movies. What can be said at this point is that play is "horizontal" in that there is not just one presentation of the moon taking place but numerous presentations together. In *The Cosmic Voyage* this horizontal aspect not only takes the form of rocket- and Earth-bound presentations of the moon happening simultaneously but also in the image of the moon "overrunning" the edges of the rocket portal. In contrast to the perfectly fitting moon of *Frau im Mond*, in Zhuravlov's film the moon exceeds the boundary of vision. This horizontal tension of representation is called experience, and it is privileged throughout the film.

[Ending] The rest of *The Cosmic Voyage* adds very little to the discussion. Most of the time on the moon is spent in stop-motion bounding from rock to rock. Professor Sedikh is lost and then found, along with a test rocket which had previously crashed, containing its still-living feline subject. The main project that the cosmonauts have on the moon is setting up a string of lights which spell out "CCCP." This signals to the earth-bound scientists, who can see it through a telescope, that the landing was successful.

One point of interest, however, lies in a scene depicting the cosmonauts finding the location in which to set up their lights. As stated above, the problem with their landing is that they have arrived on the dark side of the moon, and thus the scientists on Earth cannot see the signal they are ordered to provide as a confirmation of their arrival. Having made their way to the near side of the moon two cosmonauts see the earth for the first time from the lunar surface. While this scene has taken place in each moon movie so far, and will do so many times again, there is a slightly different element in play here. When the earth is simply shown from the lunar surface on the near side in an "objective" shot, meaning without any human figures, it is "fuzzy." However, when humans are present in a later shot, the moon takes on a new sharpness, as if coming into focus. While production issues are probably the cause of such a change, in the framework of our discussion this altering Earth takes on particular resonance. While "common sense" might dictate that this could simply be read as the earth becoming better known through the presence of a human scientific mind, the notions of being in and out of focus have been stood on their head in these films. For Méliès the moon was out-of-focus because it was unknown and waiting to be filled in with scientific understanding. In *The Cosmic Voyage* the fuzziness of the moon indicates a resistance to presentation which leads to experience. What all of these early films indicate is that a direct experience of the moon does not capture the moon at all; rather it merely points out a number of ways the moon continually eludes understanding.

Part 2: Camp

Chapter 4

Radar Men from the Moon (1952)

[Summary] *Radar Men from the Moon* (1952) is a Republic Pictures "cliffhanger" serial featuring the character Commando Cody (George Wallace), who also later appeared in *Commando Cody: Sky Marshal of the Universe* (1953). *Radar Men* is a loose sequel to the serial *King of the Rocket Men* (1949) and several of the scenes from *Radar Men* are simply culled from its predecessor, a common practice for serials of the time.[95]

The story tells of an impending invasion of Earth by the men of the moon. The earth's defenses have been under ray-gun attack as an attempt to weaken them before the invasion takes place. Commando Cody, with his flying suit, is key for foiling these evildoers. He travels to the moon and back again numerous times during the 12-episodes of the serial. The leader of the Moon Men, Retik (Roy Barcroft), has placed one of his underlings on Earth to carry out preparations for the invasion. However, a relatively small part of the serial takes place on the moon, and when it does very little attention is given to any kind of lunar experience, at least as it was developed in the previous chapter. For example, there is no attempt to represent zero gravity in space, nor the lower gravity of the moon. In fact, the only effect the travelers feel during their space flight is indicated by the way they "lean back" a bit during take-off, simulating increased g-force. What is found in place of such an experience is an extreme similarity to Earth, which is in part due to the fact that the outdoor scenes of the film were not recorded in a studio but in "the wild," meaning the Vasquez Rocks Natural Area Park in southern California; thus what makes this film seem unrealistic is the fact that its scenery is real, at least in Earth terms. On the other hand this provides an excellent opportunity to test an important idea of camp films, which is that when films are so wildly far from the truth then what truth actually remains proves to be quite interesting. This reading follows Susan Sontag's 41st thesis on camp, which is "The whole point of Camp is to dethrone the serious. Camp is playful, anti-serious. More precisely, Camp involves a new, more complex relation to 'the serious.' One can be serious about the frivolous, frivolous about the serious."[96] What is serious about the frivolity of camp films is that when absurdity strips away realism what is left is, put briefly, a horizontal tension. As Matthew Tinkcom words it in a discussion of Andy Warhol's film "Camp" (1965), the best in camp films examines "how performance, fragmented and devoted to nothing beyond itself, shifts the terrain to one of playful critique."[97] In relation to movies about the moon this idea can be restated thus: what little remains that can still be called "the moon" in these absurd representations actually indicates something essential about the lunar experience itself. Thus a number of the improbabilities of *Radar Men* will point to truths about the moon.

[Titles] In the opening titles to each episode of the serial the moon is shown three times. The first instance occurs when the title *Radar Men from the Moon* is shown, and it continues to be shown shortly thereafter. It is a still shot of the moon looking rather Earth-like since it seems to feature an atmosphere. This shot of the moon is used intermittently throughout the serial, mainly to signify a change in location from the earth to the moon: for example, it is shown after a shot on the earth, and then followed by a shot of a city on the moon, which is then followed by an interior shot within the moon city. The dark, star-filled sky surrounding the moon in this first moon shot is noticeably absent in shots of the rocket flying through space, where the sky is brightly lit. In addition, the spray of stars stretching behind the moon is obviously fantastical. This helps locate the film in the genre of "camp" since it includes obviously fantastical elements, meaning a genre which not only "loves/hates all junk equally" but also which is "ill-formed, uncontrolled, barely managing its own meanings,"[98] which is further supported by the inclusion of a miniature Saturn nestled in close to the moon. It is in this sense that *Radar Men* can be defined as camp in that out-of-date knowledge is re-vamped in a contemporary context, or, as Andrew Ross says, "The camp effect... is created not simply by a change in the mode of cultural production... but rather when the products... of a much earlier mode of production, which has lost its power to produce and dominate cultural meanings, become available, in the present, for redefinition according to contemporary codes of taste."[99]

The second and third time the moon is shown during the opening titles are very similar, they depict two different rocky terrains, although both are easily recognizable as Earth-born. Dona Jalufka and Christian Koeberl, who in their article "Moonstruck" come closest in thematic matter to the discussion here (the moon on film), describe the moon in *Radar Men* thus: "The 'lunar surface' was shot in the southwest USA, and no attempt is made to show a dark sky—normal eroded sediments and canyons with a blue sky are shown."[100] These two shots can be used to illustrate one of the central theses of camp films, which is that they are quite obviously showing what they are not. Such self-aware negation is at the heart of camp, which is, as the title of Philip Core's book on the subject indicates (in a phrase appropriated from Jean Cocteau), the lie that tells the truth.[101] At the same time these shots set the stage for what is *familiar*, for a number of following scenes involving Commando Cody flying both around Earth and across the surface of the moon are obviously filmed in very similar surroundings, if not exactly the same. This similarity is a plus for this discussion as it helps to zero in on what makes these presentations of the moon and Earth interesting. While this is taken up below, here it is worth noting that even in the opening credits the similarities between the earth and moon are beginning to bring out a truth of the moon, which is simply that it is not as strange as it seems.

[Difference] Before Commando Cody and crew leave for the moon the only direct lunar representation takes the form of a crescent moon on the communications console used by Radik to radio orders to his subordinate Krog (Peter Brocco) on Earth. Such obvious lunar signs are needed when similarities of physiology, language and setting between the earth and moon are so profuse. Thus it can be said that these obvious differences function to reinforce similarities, since they indicate how hard it can be to put difference on film. In this sense the difficulty of presenting the unknown in *Radar Men* can be related to the difficulty of knowing anything other than our own experience of the world. This is the idealist position that Meillassoux calls correlationsim, meaning that we can never know anything outside of our earthly experience because all that we know is filtered through thought.[102] However, *Radar Men* also functions differently in that such striking similarities form a taut background from which difference arises.

[Approach] Another way in which the idealist (correlationist) position takes place is that during the approach to the moon lunar images are (as in *Cosmic Voyage*) always mediated: they either appear as a drawing or through a screen on which lines of measurement are superimposed. Thus the moon is not "directly" presented, but rather the ways in which it is apprehended by human invention are shown. The first time the moon makes such an appearance is on a chart used by Commando Cody to calculate the distance to it from the earth. The chart appears in a montage of images representing the ship's journey to the moon. It simply shows both the earth and moon being illuminated by the sun along with their orbits along with a curved line representing the journey of the rocket. However, because of the manner in which the dark side of the earth is shown facing the light side of the moon an interesting relationship comes forth: once again, the celestial bodies are not as different as they seem, both are lit on the side facing the sun and dark on the side facing away. In other words, although the moon is a different celestial body, there will be many similarities between it and Earth.

[Molten Madness] The power of the moon-men is tied to their ability to control atomic power, which was a major theme for science fiction after the Second World War.[103] Therefore Commando Cody returns to the moon city to steal an atomic-powered ray-gun in order to reverse-engineer it. However, it is heavy, and he needs the help of a fellow astronaut to carry it back to his ship. On the way they are chased by a couple of moon-men in a moon-car. Commando Cody decides to hide in a cave, and this is the setting which is of interest. The moon-car is blocked by rock formations which have too small an opening for the moon car to fit through, so the moon men train a heat leaser on the cave to melt it. A number of shots follow which show the rock of the cave melting.

These shots show both rock in its solid form and rock that is molten together. The rock changes its state from solid to liquid because of the application of the moon-men's heat ray. Most of these shots show both solid and liquid states at the same time: the stillness of solidity on one side of the screen, molten mobility on the other. This is an image of horizontal tension, in that a sensual image is in conflict with its own sensual qualities. These images are due to the technique the special effects duo of the Lydecker brothers made for this scene, which involves melting a single frame of film between two plates, as Jan Hendersen describes: "Another of the other Lydeckers' signature special effects was the 'melting cave.' This effect was achieved by printing a portion of the film onto 4x5 stereopticon plates with a soft emulsion. Using heating elements placed under these plates, the emulsion runoff mimicked liquid lava."[104] This episode of the serial is entitled "Molten Terror," which indicates the importance or centrality of this effect. In addition, this indicates the interest of these "molten rock" scenes: they are dynamic, or, the rock changes state. I believe that this scene brings about an ontological truth of the moon, which has to do with time. The moon is a bright, vivid reminder that celestial bodies existed before the evolution of humans. The power of the moon-men in this scene is to bring this past state into the present. Thus the "molten" terror is the primordial soup from which all rocks, plants and animals arose. The moon-men have the power to bring this state back, just as the moon has the power to make us aware of its ancestrality.

Ben Woodard calls an awareness of this "primordial soup" which comes before humanity "slime dynamics." The reason that an awareness of such ancestral slime is important is because it indicates a world before human meaning existed. An awareness of this world before the existence of human bodies is important because it can act as a way of challenging meaning: "subtracting meaning, reducing ontological life to biological life is only to unbind pathology which seems like a far more useful weapon in combating a structure than meaning."[105] Woodard calls this thought "dark" because it is removed from our vision by time, removed from our sense of purpose because we are not a part of it, and removed from our sense of security because we are faced with both our previous and future inexistence.[106] This repetition of "removed" hints at what slime dynamics reveals, which is an awareness of the passage of time.[107] The "molten rock" shots make this passage of time visible by showing both the rock in its solid state (the present) and in molten form (the past) in the same shot. While more pedestrian reasons may be given for the inclusion of these shots in the film (they are actually culled from the episode "Molten Menace" from *King of the Rocket Men*), I argue that they bring forth not a representation of the moon, nor an experience of it, but rather the idea that the moon can engender an awareness of a time that is not ours. In this sense what is presented here is a version not only of Meillassoux's ancestrality, but more importantly of what Harman calls the "molten core" of objects, meaning the ever-shifting inner core of the what-will-always-escape-me in an object.[108] The moon is a privileged location for this "more" to take place, whether in the form of molten hiddenness or slimy ancestrality, for, as Attlee indicates, the light of the moon reminds us of a "night that was bigger than people and that dated from before their presence on the planet."[109]

[Similarity] However, at the same time what makes *Radar Men* a key film for a discussion of a camp moon is that presentations of the lunar surface are so similar to Earth. This is why it seems so fake, because it is real. Previous films used studios to film the lunar surface, a fact which lends itself to their aesthetics of a flat surface surrounded by steep wild mountains painted into an un-visitable backdrop.[110] In *Radar Men* there are of course lunar scenes shot in a studio, mainly the interiors of the moon city. And there are scenes of great artificiality, such as when the film changes locations between Moon and Earth and the earth is seen from space: the shadow of the earth model can be seen on the painted space background. However, when the actual lunar surface is seen, very little difference between it and the surface of the earth is shown. The only real difference between them is the odd bit of shrubbery.

At the same time, there is also a similarity between the two celestial bodies in terms of slime. In *Radar Men*, after the rocks are shown to return to their prior state of moltenness, a later episode shows objects on Earth taking on a similar role. In continuing their plan at disrupting the earth's defenses before they launch their invasion, the moon-men drop a bomb into a volcano to make it active and thus change weather patterns and flood a part of the planet. When the bomb explodes, similar scenes of "moltenness" are shown. In a later episode, Commando Cody is threatened by an avalanche caused by one of the moon-men firing a ray-gun. The falling rock looks quite similar to the cave scene on the moon.

However, while these images are not exactly like the molten rock of the moon cave, they all show matter transformed into a previous or alternative state by lunar weaponry. The fact that this happens both on the moon and on Earth indicates another principle of the moon: in camp, the earth and the moon get "mixed up" in that they are too similar. However, this interaction is not meant to normalize the two (as will be seen to take place in Stanley Kubrick's *2001* [1968]), but it is *political* in that it argues for "polity," meaning a version of a "community of difference" such as thought by Jean-Luc Nancy and Giorgio Agamben. Or, as Jane Burnett puts it in *Vibrant Matter*, "The political goal of a vital materialism is not the perfect equality of actants, but a polity with more channels of communication between members."[111] This presence or polity of Earth and Moon is seen in the only view of the moon shown from Earth in the serial: the light of the moon is completely surrounded by bright strokes of lightning. Here the moon is literally surrounded by an element of the earth, bringing them both together through force. The ability for force to bring about polity was seen in the way that moltenness was active on both the moon and the earth and in the way that rock and molten rock appeared together in the frame. In other words, both Earth and Moon are seen to be similar in that they are both ancestral; this horizontal similarity was brought about by seeing a kind of moltenness in them both. Thus it can be said that lunar molten terror is seen to be very earthly. The only issue is that we need the moon to be able to see it.

Chapter 5

Cat-Women of the Moon (1953)

[Summary] Released a year after *Radar Men,* Arthur Hilton's *Cat-Women of the Moon* (1953) is another camp film which manages to indirectly capture a number of truths about the moon. It tells the story of four men and a woman on a lunar expedition. On their way the woman in the group, Helen (Marie Windsor), seems to know more about the moon than is plausible, pointing out a landing site on the dark side and then knowing exactly where a large cave is located on the surface. It is later shown that she has been telepathically controlled by the surviving eight members of a race of lunar cat-women who live ensconced deep in the aforementioned cave, where the last breathable atmosphere of the moon remains. Their goal is to take over the rocket ship and go to Earth where, via the telepathic control of female earthlings, they will take over the world.

[Space] The film begins with a voice-over backed by a star field. The male voice gives the only reason provided in the film for the trip to the moon: to understand "the eternal wonders of space and time." It seems like *Cat-Women* is thus positing a similar relation-to-knowledge as found at the beginning of *Le Voyage*: the moon is unknown (represented by the "blank" space of a fuzzy chalk circle which needs to be filled in) and a trip to the moon will make it known. This "vertical" position is what is argued at the end of the voice-over: "The stars, the planets. Man has been face-to-face with them for centuries, but has barely been able to penetrate their unknown secrets. Some time, some day, the barrier will be pierced. Why must we wait? Why not now?" Thus the unknown will become known due to visiting the moon. However, this interpretation is complicated by the cut to the next scene, which is of the rocket flying through space. It does not take off from a launch pad. No crew is seen on Earth. The rocket, brightly lit, is seen and heard (with a loud roar) hurtling through pitch-black space (Figure 2).

Figure 2. *Cat-Women of the Moon* (1953).

In this sense the earth does not occupy a point of comparison as it did in *Radar Men*: the moon is on its own in this film, and what happens on it is left to the realm of fantasy.

However, this interpretation is a not-quite accurate reading of the film. During take-off the earth *is* shown. It is seen through the rocket's single window. However, it is shown speeding by outside the window, and at first it is difficult to ascertain exactly what is being presented. As discussed earlier, *acceleration* was used to frame the way that the coordinates of a system could be followed to such an extent that the system itself would become dislocated. This was seen in connection with presentations of the moon. However, here it is seen in connection with the earth, and it is seen at the very beginning of the film, before any other image of Earth has been shown. What does this mean in the context of our discussion? I argue that this is an image of an unimportant earth. By this I mean that the earth is shown speeding toward its own uselessness. In fact, it is so distorted that it looks as barren as the moon. This "negation" of the earth is why the rocket is shown only in space, and never on Earth: there is no point, it is useless. While voices from Earth are heard in the ship in the form of radio contact, no image is ever matched to these voices. Thus the earthlings remain in a state of suspension. It is true that the earth is shown twice in the film from the surface of the moon. However, it will be seen that these scenes are couched within a context of enjoying the moon itself rather than any kind of contact with a notion of "home."

[Mobile Moon] Arrival is indicated by seeing the moon from outside the rocket window. What is unusual about this scene is the movement of the moon: as the astronauts sit and discuss the landing the moon moves around in an inexplicable manner: first from left to extreme right, then from extreme right to left, before eventually moving down. All of this takes place while the astronauts barely notice the moon. In fact, the commander of the expedition, Laird (Sonny Tufts), only notices the moon when it first appears, and then only with a quick glance. He does not

Figure 3. *Cat-Women of the Moon* (1953).

comment on it. Otherwise, he spends his time talking to Helen. And no one else takes any notice of the presence of the erratic lunar disc either (Figure 3).[112]

So what is going on with the moon here? As Laird and Helen are talking it moves around behind their backs: left, right, over and down. In this sense the moon is a camp moon in that, as Tinkcom says, "narrative fails as an explanation for how a given text is formally and aesthetically conceived" and "the film image has diverged from *narrative* expectations"[113] into bad taste. This indicates one of the key structures of this chapter, which is one of *slipperiness* and *divergence* and it will be found in both the moon and the construction of Woman. Yet the moon is also being *ignored* by two astronauts, and seen *through the medium of a rocket window* not by the passengers of the rocket but by the viewers of the film. This scene thus does two things: 1) it places the moon "outside" the thought of the astronauts (since they do not pay much attention to it) and 2) it places the moon squarely within the thought or experience of the viewer.

Let's take these events in order. The first shows that when the moon is not observed it does strange things. The movements of left, right and down are odd because they have no matched action on the side of the rocket ship, meaning that the movement of the moon is not shown to be due to the movement of the ship; instead, the moon is just moving around on its own. The reason for the moon's movements does not lie within any known laws of physics; instead they are farcical. Rather than bringing forth a physical truth of the moon, this movement foregrounds an ontological truth. This idea has already been presented a number of times. For example, in *Le Voyage* the moon was presented horizontally, in a number of different fashions: on a blackboard, as a face, as a theatrical set. It was argued that the appearance of all these different presentations within the same film showed that they did not "exhaust" what the moon means in any way but rather their inadequacy at presenting the moon indicates something important about the moon itself. This inexhaustible something-important cannot be presented. These are, as Harman describes them, "vacuum-sealed objects withdrawing from all relations."[114] However, a key problem immediately becomes apparent: if things are sealed off, how do they ever affect each other? In other words, if the moon can never be presented, then what are we doing with presentations of the moon? Each chapter has attempted to answer this question in a different manner: looking at the gap between subjects and objects, indirectness, and the mechanics of slime. What *Cat-Women* adds to the mix is to add a cultural element not only found in this film but also in a number of others we have looked at, and that is the function of women in the lunar landscape. Put differently, I argue that the cultural function of women in *Cat-Women* has a structural counterpart which can be used to develop the manner in which, as offensive as it may sound at first, sealed-off objects interact with the world.

However, at this point it is important to note that there is a disruptive moment in this scene of the mobile moon, an image which I have ignored until now. In the middle of the moon's messing about, it is shown in an exterior shot, as a whole, and independent of the rocket ship. This means that another moon is presented in between or within these shots of the "weird" mobile moon. This shot acts a reminder that the mobile moon is just one in the plethora of lunar presentations. It locates both itself and the shots of the moon moving around on the rocket screen in relation to each other rather than one or the other in relation to an original moon. In other words, the moon is both all of these parts and more than these parts, at least in this horizontal presentation. Harman illustrates the "more" of these parts in a discussion of the image of a zebra he sees on a banner outside a window: "the zebra can be both substance and aggregate at the same time. It is something over and above its pieces, for it has qualities that these pieces do not have, and not every change in these pieces transforms the zebra itself."[115] Above this was called horizontal tension. In *Cat-Women* the mechanism for the way that the "more" of horizontal tension comes forth is called Woman.

[Woman] The first woman who appears in the film is Helen. She is a part of the scientific team on the rocket, heading navigation. However, although she is dressed in a similar manner to the rest of the crew, she is also differentiated, as Marie Lathers argues in *Space Oddities: Women and Outer Space in Popular Film and Culture*: "Although from the 1950s to the 70s there were certainly instances of women wearing fairly realistic space suits, these were rare. Helen in *Cat-Women* does, but she is outnumbered by the rest of the crew—even when a woman does wear an outfit, the emphasis is still on the man in the suit."[116] This difference is also seen in the characterization of the female-on-board. Upon waking up from their induced sleep during take-off, the male crew gathers to strategize while Helen fixes her make-up and hair. In addition the first thing she does is confess a strange feeling of déjà-vu, the strangeness of which increases when each of the crew members relate a greeting message back to Earth, with Helen's being simply: "Hello Alpha, we are on our way." Alpha (Carol Brewster), we are to learn, is no one on Earth but is the lead cat-woman on the moon; the oddness of Helen's utterance is emphasized here by the blank stares of the rest of the crew and Helen's own blank face while she says it.

In fact, in the scene of the "mobile moon" discussed above Helen relates mysterious knowledge of a landing site to Laird. She has received this information through a telepathic connection made by the lunar cat-women. However, the strange thing is not just that she has such a detailed knowledge of localities on the moon but also that her landing site is to be found on the dark side, of which no images have been taken and no knowledge obtained. Thus Helen functions as a "link" between human knowledge and that which lies outside of it—she is a conduit between vacuum-sealed objects and an experience of such objects, just as she functions as a conduit between the thoughts of the cat-women and the actions of the rocket ship. The reason Helen is able to function in such a way is twofold: first an intrinsic reason, she is a woman, and thus the cat-women are able to communicate with her and only her in this way; but then an extrinsic reason for control is provided, for once the astronauts land on the moon and begin exploring the cave in which the cat-women live, one of the cat-women assaults Helen and traces a moon on her hand by which she can be controlled.

This secondary form of control seems superfluous, for the cat-women were already able to control Helen from afar without such a sign. In addition, the moon-mark itself is superfluous in the way that it was filmed: the round disc is superimposed on the hand rather than drawn on it or created with make-up (Figure 4).

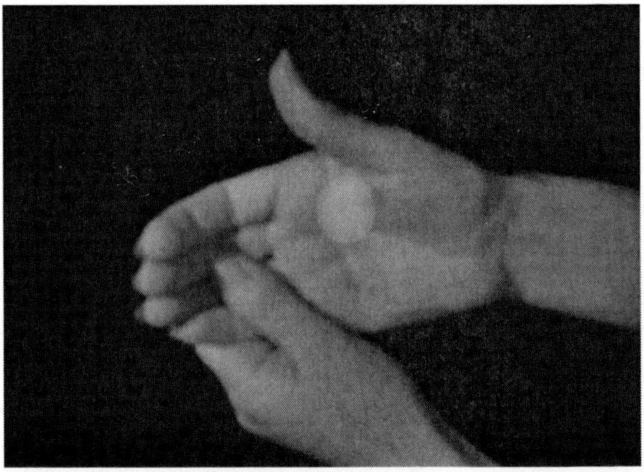

Figure 4. *Cat-Women of the Moon* (1953).

This superimposition is superfluous because the movements of the disc are not well-matched with the movements of the hand, and thus the moon disc is "mobile" in a manner similar to the moon in the rocket window. I call this motion superfluous because it does not "mean" anything within the story; it is a mistake, part of the camp elements of the film. However, it is these "superfluous" moments which tie together two different elements of the film, as offensive as it may sound: woman and the moon. While connections between woman and the moon have a long history,[117] our work is to delineate what mechanism binds Woman and Moon in the film.

[Feminism] One way to approach this topic is to see if a discussion of women in film can be transposed into a discussion of the moon in film. This can be attempted by taking a citation from a canonical feminist text on film and seeing if it can be usurped into a lunar discussion. Mary Ann Doane's *Femmes Fatales: Feminism, Film Theory, Psychoanalysis* describes the ontological function of the femme fatale in (mainly) American film noir in a manner similar to the way in which the moon is being developed here. By substituting the moon for a specific kind of woman, the femme fatale (and it for her), in a key passage, we come up with the following text:

> Because the moon's representation is so dependent upon perceptual ambiguity and ideals about the limits of vision in relation to knowledge, its incarnation in the cinema is a particularly telling one. Because it seems to confound power, subjectivity, and agency with the very lack of these attributes, its relevance to feminist discourses is critical. Since feminisms are forced to search out symbols from a lexicon that does not exist, their acceptance of the moon as a sign of strength in an unwritten history must also and simultaneously involve an understanding and assessment of all the epistemological baggage the moon carries along with it.[118]

While the elements of this passage which "match" this discussion of the moon are telling, the elements which do not are even more so.

In the first sentence what seems most moon-like is "perceptual ambiguity" and "limits of vision in relation to knowledge." The first phrase relates to the "indirectness" which was discussed in the first chapter. If we take ambiguity to mean multiple meanings of a single signifier and perceptual to mean perceiving a representation, then the multiple representations of the moon presented together in *Le Voyage* seems like a prime illustration of this idea. For example, when the rocket lands in the eye of the Moon Man and then lands once again on the planet surface, a horizontal ambiguity arises as to how to read these two diverse yet synchronous presentations of a moon landing. However, the second half of the sentence, which foregrounds cinema as the privileged locus for the figure of the femme fatale, has not been taken into account so far in this discussion. The privileged role of cinema in this sense comes to the fore in part four of this book which focuses on the actual footage taken on the moon during the Apollo missions.

Coming back to Doane's appropriated text, in the beginning of the second sentence the agency of the femme fatale/moon is posited. According to Doane the function of such ambiguity it is to "confound power, subjectivity, and agency." Translated into the language of this text, various and simultaneous representations of the moon confound idealist notions of subjects trapped inside a world of thought. While the result of this confoundedness is perhaps even antithetical to what Doane posits, there seems to be some agreement as to the power of an instable image.

The end of this passage calls for feminism both to take the moon seriously as an object of study and to respect the history that comes with it. One of the main figures which tangle with feminism in Doane's book is the femme fatale of her title. There are a number of ways in which Doane's reading of the femme fatale overlaps with the reading of the moon being presented here, although there are also a number of key differences which point to areas which need further exploration in this study.

However, it would be of interest to see if 1) there are further parallels in Doane's text with the moon and 2) if there are parallels with Doane's thought in other speculative materialist discussions.

Regarding the first point, Doane's discussion of King Vidor's *Gilda* (1946) focuses on the way that the femme fatale both is and is not cinematic, which addresses the second half of the first sentence of the previous quote, which has been twisted into asking what is cinematic about the moon. Doane argues that "In the classical Hollywood text, knowledge is generally supported by the image, which ultimately acts as a guarantee of the reality-effect of the film. Individual characters may lie, but the image does not." The figure of the femme fatale Gilda (Rita Hayworth) "lacks credibility" and thus challenges the realism of the image. This challenge is performed via "a proliferation of points of view, a multiplication of the means whereby the spectator is given access to knowledge."[119] Transferring this thought to the moon, it can be said that the moon is in a position in which its multiple presentations challenge the truth of its presentation. This seems to be the "natural" place of the moon in these films as none has presented a solidified picture of the moon throughout its run-time. However, this notion of multiplicity will be challenged in the next two parts of the book, with films including a more realistic portrayal of the moon and of actual footage shot on the moon. The multiplicity of these images will not lie in a lack of realism but elsewhere.

[Multiple] The idea of the ontological validity of multiplicity can be found in Meillassoux's literary study *The Number and the Siren: A Decipherment of Mallarmé's* Coup de Dés. In this text Meillassoux adopts the antiquated approach of finding a code within Mallarmé's poem which explains the whole. He eventually succeeds in this by counting the total words in the poem and coming up with a total of 707, a number which he then uses to interpret the content of the poem. His main argument is that 707 represents a metrical form which is so peculiar that it can only exist once, thus indicating the idiosyncratic nature of the work. However, what is of interest here is the way in which 707 both is and is not the count of the poem. Meillassoux ends his book by showing how other counts are possible, including 705, 714 and 703.[120] One of the tasks of Meillassoux's book is to take this multiplicity of codes seriously: "As that which makes no longer *being*, but the *perhaps*, the first task—the task to come—of thinkers and poets."[121]

Both Meillassoux and Doane foreground the perhaps in the form of instability. This is the connection between Woman and Moon in *Cat-Women*: they are interchangeable because both have a similar function, they show the truth in the untruth of the stable image. This is nothing new. The instability of the image of "woman" was seen in the way that Helen is an unknown element to her crew members because she functions as a conduit for the thoughts of others. The instability of the image is shown to be true in terms of the moon in the way that the "mobile moon" is moved by a force which has no counterpart in either the reality of the view or the reality of the film. This connection dangerously aligns Woman with "disruption," the disentanglement of which is one of the aims of Doane's book.[122] However, *Cat-Women* problematizes this association in an important way: Woman/Moon does not just disrupt Man/Earth, rather both are transformed when they appear together.

[Light and Dark] The relationship between Earth and Moon, or between Man and Woman, is projected onto that between light and dark. The way that light and dark problematize the notion of Woman (dark) as disruption is that light takes on strange properties on the moon. According to the logic of the film, the near side of the moon is seen as fatally hot while on the dark side illuminated objects suffer no such fate. This is problematic because both sides of the moon actually receive sunlight (the dark or far side during the new moon) so the light on both sides is the same, that of the sun (or of sunlight reflected off the earth's surface, or earthshine). However, on the near side the light is deadly and on the far side it simply illuminates.

An example of fatal light can be seen shortly after the astronauts land on the moon. When on the rocket, Helen telepathically receives the landing location from the cat-women and the rest of the crew is shocked that it is on the dark side since there is no data available about the far side of the moon, and so landing there has been judged too dangerous. However, once they do land on the dark side Laird shows how even walking on the light side is impossible because of the extreme heat. He illustrates this by putting a cigarette on the light side and showing how it immediately bursts into flames. Thus an aesthetic of the moon is established in which demarcations of light and dark become important. For example, when the ship lands it is shown being on the dark side and when Helen indicates their destination for exploration, a cave which is shown to house the cat-women's city, it is also seen to lie in shadow.

Thus the moon of this film is necessarily a dark moon, for safety's sake. However, once this is established another important element of the relationship between dark and light begins to come forth: illuminated elements do appear on the dark side, but the illumination is not dangerous. All the objects lit in this manner, however, are Earth-bound or -born, including the rocket ship and the astronauts, both harmlessly illuminated on the dark side despite the cigarette experiment.

Therefore in one sense a simple idea is being presented: light on the earth is safe while light on the moon is dangerous. However, when the light enters the dark side of the moon as a non-dangerous element it indicates something else, which is, in the least, that in the movie light can "shift" from being dangerous to safe for no other reason than that lunar light is strange. The light is not disruptive but rather "mobile" in a way similar to the moon outside the rocket window. This is because its effects "shift" even when the object stays the same.

[Face-to-Face] This shifting also takes place in different contexts, which can be seen in comparing the composition of two important scenes in the film with each other. In the scene of the mobile moon, Helen and Laird are seen talking to each other on the rocket ship. They are sitting below the porthole, not noticing the moon's rapid flight around the edges of the window. The composition of this scene finds a similarity in Figure 5, in which Alpha explains all about the cat-women to Helen.

Figure 5. *Cat-Women of the Moon* (1953).

While both are simply medium shots featuring two people talking, there are deeper connections between the two. First, Alpha looks at Helen's imprinted palm-moon and then confirms "you are one of us, ask anything." Helen's first question is one of mixed-states: she is unsure "if you're speaking my language or I yours." It is explained that although the cat-women can speak telepathically they have chosen to speak English with Helen, although they also know all the other languages of Earth. This knowledge comes from the fact that the cat-women have had a lot of time to study, since their generation "predates" Helen's by centuries. In fact, as they explain elsewhere, the cat-woman race is 20 million years old, putting them in the category of ancestrality. At the same time, there are elements that were identified as being connected to the notion of the femme fatale. This can be seen in the end of the scene when the cat-women reveal their plan. Because they can only control women telepathically, they need to use other methods to control the men and get them to explain the workings of the rocket so that Helen and three cat-women can travel back to Earth and dominate it. One of the cat-women says that they will need to know the men's weaknesses. Helen, under the influence of the moon, says "Strange, I should care what happens to them, and yet I don't." Alpha replies, "You see, we don't care, and you are one of us." Hence the "fatale" of the femme fatale comes forth.

However, there is a more vital structural connection between these two shots. Instead of just seeing the similarities on the level of theme or content, the form of their respective compositions brings together Woman and Moon, but in a more complex fashion. To elude a lengthy description a brief sketch will outline the most important nodes of interpretation:

	Mobile Moon			Light Statue		Dark Statue
					Candle	
Laird		Helen		Alpha		Helen

The diagram illustrates that on the rocket ship it is the unobserved yet mobile moon which casts a central influence on the action while on the planet there is a more mixed approach. In the latter the light of the statue, a feature connected with Earth, hangs over Alpha, while the dark of the other statue, a feature connected with the moon, hangs over Helen. In the middle lies a candle, perhaps representing a celestial body, probably the moon or sun. On the other hand the flame of the candle represents the kind of control that the cat-women have over nature (similar to the atomic power of the moon-men of *Radar Men*), for in an earlier scene they are shown extinguishing a flame with the power of their minds. If this latter interpretation is privileged, then it can be argued that an ontological truth of the moon lies in an ability to "mix up" or shift objects on the level of presentation. In other words, the slipperiness of the moon is reflected in a slipperiness of "things on Earth," or in our phenomenological reality, much as the "moltenness" of the moon in *Radar Men* was also seen on Earth. This idea is taken even further, and more literally, in the next film under discussion, *Nude on the Moon* (1961). For while in *Cat-Women* the moon has the power to shift, in *Nude* it has the power to liberate.

Chapter 6

Nude on the Moon (1961)

[Summary] *Nude on the Moon* is a camp film made by Doris Wishman in 1961. It tells the story of two rocket scientists, Jeff (Lester Brown) and the Professor (William Mayer), who make the first journey to the moon. While preparing their ship in the lab their secretary Cathy (Marietta) confesses her feelings for Jeff to the older Professor. The latter explains that Jeff is focused on science and has no thought of romance. When the pair finally land on the moon they find it mainly inhabited by topless women (with a few men included). The Queen of these women is played by the same actress as the secretary, although neither Jeff nor the Professor notices the similarity on the moon. Jeff falls in love with her but both the Professor and the Queen know that he has to return to Earth, mainly because the earthmen only have a 13-hour supply of oxygen with them. Upon returning to Earth

Figure 6. *Nude on the Moon* (1961). With permission from Something Weird, www.somethingweird.com.

Jeff is forlorn because of his lost love. However, when he sees Cathy he recognizes her as the Queen he fell in love with on the moon and the two embrace.

[Earth-Moon] The opening titles of the film sets the key in romance. An original tune by Ralph Young is sung over a static shot of the earth seen from the moon surface (Figure 6).

It is only after the first minute or so of the song that the first title appears. The credits thus set out one of the key elements of this film, which is a development of the relation between the earth and the moon. The beginning of the film offers a cheesy meditation on this relation by showing this scene with no titles for over a minute, just letting the music play over the image. The moon surface is seen to be of a similar darkness to that of space while the earth is presented in rich color up in the sky. The fact that the film opens with a view of the earth from the moon indicates that the moon is going to change or influence a reading of the earth.

This theory receives almost too-literal support from the end of the film, when the same shot is shown and the same song is played. Yet there is a difference: color. In the opening credits both Earth and Moon are given a blue tint, while at the end of the film they are given a green one. Although what these two colors represent is indicated below, what is for certain at this point is that there is an important change between these two shots since the same shot could have easily been used both times. What is interesting is that this color change has taken place on *both* the earth and the moon: both places have altered, and in the same way (they are both now green). Thus the opening of the film does not emphasize a change in the presentation of the earth brought about by a visit to the moon but rather a change in the relation of both objects to each other. This "dual change" is reflected in a number of other moments in the film.

[Fake Moon] The first time the moon makes an appearance in the diegesis of the film it is as a fake moon. Jeff and the Professor enter their rocket for take-off. The next shot seems to be of the bright "fuzzy" white moon in a dark starless sky. This image of the moon seems to indicate that the rocket trip would then fill in this blank disc with scientific knowledge. This matches some of the previous dialogue in the lab between Jeff and the Professor, which is actually some of the most realistic dialogue of its type to appear so far in the lunar films under discussion. However, this hypothesis is shown to be false; the fuzzy moon is a red herring. Actually, it is the window of the door to the rocket ship which is soon opened. Thus *Nude* indicates its removal from the goal of creating a scientific moon by filling in the fuzziness. Part of the definition of camp films is that they "know" they are camp, which is what this camera trick indicates. In other words, another economy is in play in which actual truths about the moon are to come about through its fantastic representation.

[Face-Off] After the initial take-off the Professor matter-of-factly says to Jeff "Now let's have a look at the earth." A scope on the instrument panel is foregrounded before a cut to the earth, indicating the means by which the earth is seen. The image of the earth shows a smooth sphere with a representation of some of the continents in relief. Rotating in front of a star field, apparently without any axial tilt, this simple model is yet another reminder of the genre in which we find ourselves. However, what happens next is a first in lunar films. Without voice over or cutaway this shot dissolves into an image of the moon. First the whole screen starts turning blue and then the greenness of the moon, which is so large that it exceeds the frame, takes over.

There are a number of elements involved in this dissolve: the earth and the moon are structured as "facing" each other because the change in point of view is not matched with any action on the rocket ship; in a similar vein, no comments are made in a voice over from anyone on the ship, nor is this change reflected on when the action returns to the astronauts in the sense that they do not comment on it; in addition, the moon is larger than the earth, although of course in reality it is much smaller; and finally, the shift in color from blue to green mirrors the change that takes place in the moonscape view of the earth in the opening and closing credits of the film. Rather than treating these elements individually I am interested in what ties them together; as appropriate for a film about lunar nudists, the answer lies in the *erotic*.

[The Erotic] The erotic can be thought of as a way of relating rather than something necessarily sexual. As Laura Marks develops in *Touch*, "Eroticism arrives in the way a viewer engages with this surface and in a dialectical movement between the surface and the depth of the image."[123] This "movement" is described as depending "on a tension between the sense of control and submission on the part of each person, rather than complete domination on one side and complete submission on the other."[124] It is this *mutual tension* of the erotic which can be seen in the dissolve between the earth and the moon in *Nude*. While a dissolve usually implies a passage of time, in this case it is a means for joining together disparate objects. For a classic example of the former we can cite the "dissolve" Sergei Eisenstein was surprised to find in Charles Dickens' novel *A Tale of Two Cities* (1859). Eisenstein quotes from the beginning of the final chapter of the novel, picking a description of six two-wheeled carts carrying wine: "Six tumbrils roll along the streets. Change these back again to what they were, thou powerful enchanter, Time, and they shall be seen to be the carriages of absolute monarchs, the equipages of feudal nobles, the toilettes of flaring Jezebels, the churches that are not my father's house but dens of thieves, the huts of millions of starving peasants!"[125] What makes this narrative description a dissolve in Eisenstein's reading is the element of time, which is addressed in the form of apostrophe (thou Time!). Thus the mechanism of the dissolve becomes a temporal displacement. But another reading of Dickens' passage illuminates a different mechanism. The second sentence begins with the imperative "Change..." The address of this imperative is unknown. It lies in the future. So until the reader comes across Time in the sentence it is *change* which is foregrounded. I argue that change is the medium of Marks' mutual tension.[126]

In *Nude* time is not the focus of the dissolve. Before the moon is shown the Professor suggests they both take a look at it. When the film "returns" to the rocket the change in view receives no comment of any kind. The scientists are busy with other tasks. While the dissolve could represent the Professor "changing" the view of the scope to see the moon, this is also problematic; since the astronauts did not comment on this change of view it would mean that only the view of the earth is worthy of an utterance while a view of the object of their mission would be uninteresting. Thus other avenues open for interpretation. There is a certain ambiguity to the dissolve when a matching action is removed as the film returns to the rocket. What becomes foregrounded is similar to what is foregrounded in the passage from Dickens: when Time is removed from the equation then change is what remains. Thus an issue with Marks is highlighted: her reading of the erotic seems to foreground the collapse of difference between what she calls the surface and the depth of the image. What seems to be happening here is not a collapse of difference but rather the presencing of difference. So further reading of the erotic is required.

[S/M] Marks anchors the above quote on the erotic in a discussion of the use of S/M in gay pornography, thus her focus on the tension between submission and control. While Marks engages an interesting direction here, the focus of the dissolve in *Nude* seems to lie in foregrounding change rather than collapsing the time between different shots. Thus the importance of color in the dissolve: the change from blue to green takes place before enough information is given to understand that this is a dissolve from the earth to the moon. A similar change in focus takes place when Steven Shaviro, in *The Cinematic Body*, contrasts Masochism to S/M. Shaviro, in a reading of Gilles Deleuze's *Masochism*, states that the theoretical strength of the figure of the masochist is that "The masochist seeks not to reach a final consummation, but to hold it off, to prolong the frenzy, for as long as possible."[127] The dissolve in *Nude* is a "holding off" and "prolonging" of the change from Earth to Moon and thus it is a foregrounding of the same operation of change. This position is masochistic in that it is painful: it is hard not knowing what is being represented. And it can be the position of cinema itself: "Cinema seduces its viewers by mimetically exacerbating erotic tension, in an orgy of unproductive expenditure. Visual fascination is a direct consequence of this masochistic heightening, rather than of any secondary movements of suturing and satiation."[128] This tension is "held off" in that when the rocket does land on the moon the colored confusion continues. It is in moments of being held-off that change can take place, since where one is going next is not foreclosed.

When the rocket lands in *Nude* the color-coding continues. The whole lunar scene is green, which is the color used to symbolize the moon in the dissolve, but in the sky a celestial body is seen, which would supposedly be the earth, but which takes on the appearance of a half-moon because of being half-lit. In this scene the appearance of Earth is held-off by looking too much like the moon. Yet the rest of *Nude* offers an opposite mechanism for creating such confusion: rather than holding back, everything is shown; thus the importance of *nudity*.

[Surface] The main point of *Nude* is showing women nude from the waist-up. This is a key camp element of the film. At the same time, it is the main filmic indicator that action is taking place on the moon and not the earth, thus it is one of the few differences between the celestial bodies which marks where the action happens. I believe that this nudity has, besides titillation, an ontological role to play. It is different than the other markers of lunar difference in the film. For example, although when the astronauts exit the rocket they are seen as backed by a light sky reminiscent of *Radar Men*, this is quickly followed by two shots representing a more typical representation of the lunar surface, dark and sparse. The darkness of these images matches the more realistic moon of the dissolve and they reflect an attempt at matching the scientific banter between the two scientists before take-off with visual representations after landing. However, these attempts are soon replaced with the kind of images of the moon which remain throughout the film, in which the lunar surface looks like southern Florida, where the film was shot (Figure 7).

Figure 7. *Nude on the Moon* (1961). With permission from Something Weird, www.somethingweird.com.

In keeping with the scientific discourse between the astronauts, the Floridian landscape is explained away by assuming they have landed inside a crater which is unobservable by Earth-bound telescopes. Thus they are not a part of the logic of the "telescopic" moon which attempts to provide more and more accurate presentations of the moon as technologies of vision advance. In fact they confront this knowledge directly when they say that "The largest telescopes have always pictured the moon as barren." There is even a question of whether they have arrived on the moon at all. Faced with the Earth-like conditions, Jeff asks "How do we know it is the moon, Professor?" The Professor answers in an odd manner. He taps the outer shell of the rocket and says, a bit unsure of himself, "Well, it's got us here."

However, even this seemingly concrete assurance that they are on the moon is questioned at the end of the film. After returning to Earth Jeff talks to the Professor on the phone about getting funding for their next mission. The Professor says that funding has been denied because experts have looked over the rocket and they say that there is no evidence that the rocket has ever been to space, let alone that it could ever get off the ground in the first place. This leaves Jeff, who is still dazed by falling in love with the Moon Queen, in a conundrum. He says, "The Moon? We don't really know where we went." In one sense this posits the landing on the moon as a dream, which is supported by the astronauts falling asleep on the way there, supposedly caused by the increased g-force involved in take-off and landing. What is more interesting is that instead of just making it all a dream sequence, the movie negates the necessity of their having been on any kind of "real" moon at all; perhaps what they landed on was a camp moon. In this sense the comments on the film by Jalufka and Koeberl are spot-on, but not in the manner in which they intended: "It is hard to determine whether the director was trying to parody past SciFi films, or if this was a misguided attempt at serious filmmaking."[129] It is both. This lack of seriousness can function as parody while the self-awareness of its own absurdity can function as seriousness.

In this sense the initial differences from the earth that are experienced by the astronauts are so obviously non-lunar in origin that they are not taken seriously. For example, an everyday-looking bush is described as "A very interesting specimen," and to stress its strangeness the "readings" from a "reader" are commented upon; then a chunk of gold is found just lying on the ground near a pond (Figure 7). These minor differences are of no import to the construction of the moon in the film, a theory which gets support from the fact that all samples, along with photos, are lost before the astronauts return to Earth. Instead, what is important is the way their experience on the moon is different from their experience of everyday life on Earth. This difference is first posited in a number of standard ways for moon films, such as with shots of the earth and moon from the rocket window; however, the main difference is that the people on the moon are naked.

[Nudity] When the astronauts are looking at bushes and gold found in the grass, the way in which these scenes are shot does not call attention to itself. These are mainly wide shots attempting zero focalization. However, when the astronauts observe the inhabitants of the moon their specific location while taking a look is often marked. At first they are looking over the edge of a sculpture of a crescent moon[130] and later, in a shot much repeated, they are filmed from below while standing on top a low hill, taking pictures of the goings-on around them, sometimes even shooting from the crotch (Figure 8).

In this sense the astronauts are shown seeing (through matched action) rather than just looking (at the ground or at a bush, with no matched action). Thus the subjects are positioned in relation to what they see in a way that is different from how they observe the bush and gold. What the astronauts see are a number of topless men and women going about various non-

Figure 8. *Nude on the Moon* (1961). With permission from Something Weird, www.somethingweird.com.

productive activities such as spinning each other around on a stone disc, taking in the sun and pretending to have mustaches like the Professor.

These scenes show that rather than finding gold or bush-anomalies, the most important difference between the moon and the earth is skin. Naturism entered the US during the 1930s through Germany,[131] and it was during the time that *Nude* was made that this relatively naïve form of naturism gained a political edge in the sexual revolution.[132] *Nude* belongs to the former group, featuring an innocence which is a part of much of the early work of the film's director and driving force, Doris Wishman. Her films were "ersatz documentaries taking place in nudist camps" which could show nudity because of their documentary nature. They were "showing ample amounts of both male and female nudity, yet remaining very innocent as the movies were strictly sex-free."[133] In this sense *Cat-Women* was more sexual than *Nude* in that it featured scenes of seduction and even a kiss on the moon.[134] Here the function of nudity on the moon lies elsewhere than in "mere" arousal, although as Shaviro has argued appeals to the "baser" emotions can be a productive manner of challenging the dominance of psychological approaches to film theory.[135] I argue for a different function for nudity in the film, which is similar to that of the dissolve in the Earth-Moon face-off: nudity simply represents change rather than one state (clothed) or another (not).

The first step in this argument is to see how nudity relates to Shaviro's reading of masochism as a "putting-off." As quoted above, Shaviro sees masochism as cinematic because it can lead to "an orgy of unproductive expenditure." This unproductiveness is seen not just in the way in which the Moon Dolls "do nothing" all day except lounge around (Figure 9) but also in the way in which they treat the astronauts, which is, in general, of a mild detachment..

Figure 9. *Nude on the Moon* (1961). With permission from Something Weird, www.somethingweird.com.

Thus masochism has a structural relationship to camp, certain forms of which, as Andrew Ross says, involve the "re-creation of surplus value from forgotten forms of labor."[136]

The nonchalant attitudes of the women on the moon are seen when the Professor and Jeff are first discovered by some of the few men on the moon. The astronauts are immediately jailed but are soon set free by the Moon Queen/Secretary, much to the dismay of the other Selenites. However, once free, they are left undisturbed just to walk around and explore, with only a few moments of interest from the Moon Dolls relating to their strange clothing. Thus each side displays a kind of visual fascination with each other which has no real end other than looking, which is an example of Shaviro's reading of unproductive expenditure. This is true at least until Jeff falls in love with the Queen at the end of the film and wants to stay as long as he can with her, no matter that it will shortly end in his demise (although she then "puts him off" by insisting he return to Earth). While Shaviro argues this "visual fascination" is a part of the inclusion of "putting-off" figures in cinema, I would take the argument a step further and posit that such putting-off makes the relation between the two objects being put off visible.

Giorgio Agamben begins his essay "Nudity" with a discussion of a series of performances by Vanessa Beecroft in which a number of women stand naked together in a gallery-articulated space. Agamben states that "The first impression of those who attempted to observe not only the women but also the visitors was that this was a nonplace. *Something that could have, and perhaps, should have happened did not take place.*"[137] For Agamben nudity is a nonplace because it is an *event*. His location of why this is so in Catholic theology is less important here than the way in which nudity "is the obscure presupposition of the addition of a piece of clothing or the sudden result of its removal—an unexpected gift or an unexpected loss—nudity belongs to time and history, not to being and form. We can therefore only experience nudity as a denudation and a baring, never as a form and a stable possession. At any rate, it is difficult to grasp and impossible to hold on to."[138] While the "impossible to hold on to" in this quote relates to Shaviro's "holding off," Agamben seems to be re-inserting time into this discussion when the reading of the Earth/Moon dissolve attempted to take it out. I believe that this is an important point that draws out a key difference between *Nude* and the work under discussion in Agamben's essay. Agamben discusses Beecroft's performances, in which real models who are almost totally naked (sometimes wearing high heels or pantyhose) are "forced" to hold their positions for long periods of time, an aspect of her work which has garnered criticism.[139] These models are not always nude: presumably they get dressed in the morning before they come to the gallery and get dressed after their work is done in the evening. Thus a sense of gifting or time is essential to the performance. The Moon Dolls of *Nude* are different, however. Although only topless, they have always been and always will be topless. There is no other state of being-clothed for them; thus there is no sense of time involved in their nudity, it is "a form and a stable possession." However, it still remains "ungraspable." This latter element can be seen in the end of the film, when the secretary Cathy and the Moon Queen are shown to be one, through yet another dissolve.

[Nude on Earth] When the astronauts have only one hour of air left the Professor decides it is time to get back to the rocket ship. Jeff, who entertained no room for romance on Earth, has no room for science on the moon: he is ready to give up his life and work to spend his last hour with the Moon Queen. Lucky for Jeff, both the Professor and the Moon Queen convince him to return to the ship, which he does. However, in their haste the astronauts lose all evidence of their being on the moon. Back on Earth, this leads to the scene described above when their ever being on the moon is put in question. After this conversation Cathy enters the room where Jeff is. She just stands there, saying nothing. Jeff also does not speak. Then the camera zooms in on the secretary and goes out of focus. While out of focus there is a switch and the secretary is shown to be the Moon Queen, topless and with her antenna (Figure 10).

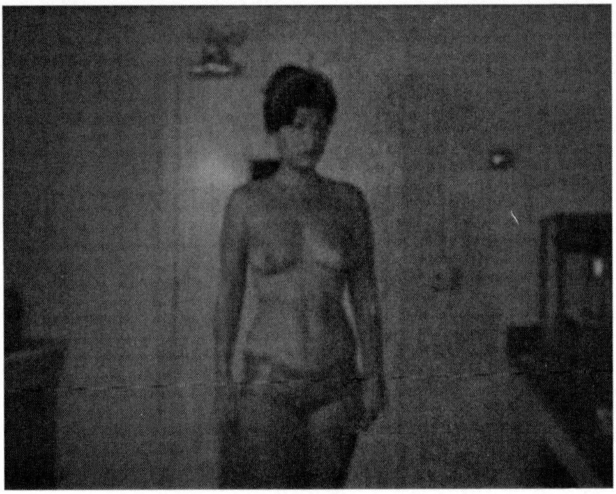

Figure 10. *Nude on the Moon* (1961). With permission from Something Weird, www.somethingweird.com.

The camera then comes back into focus and cuts to Jeff, who licks his lips. Then there is a cut back to the Moon Queen and the process is reversed: out of focus, cut to secretary, then back in focus. Then Jeff and the secretary embrace. The Professor enters the room, unnoticed, sees what they are doing, and discretely exits. The two continue their silent embrace and the movie ends.

The point of this scene is not to prove that the astronauts were on Earth the whole time, or that Jeff needed a romantic fantasy to become aware of his feelings for Cathy,[140] but rather that it does not matter whether they were ever on the moon at all, because the earth and the moon are the same. This is what nudity exposes, that there is "nothing there." This is also a key difference that Harman sees between himself and Meillassoux: while Meillassoux sees the moon as an example of ancestrality, Harman reads it as an object that is never knowable. As Harman argues, "Supposedly the moon is sitting there before us, exhaustively knowable because its primary qualities can be mathematized. My point was, and still is, that *no amount of knowledge of the moon ever turns into a moon*."[141] For Harman the knowledge about the moon points to how the moon resists that knowledge, exists apart from that knowledge, and is thus an object which exits outside thought (and which we can only know indirectly). This is also the lesson of camp: the moon in films like *Radar Men*, *Cat-Women* and *Nude* has almost nothing to do with the moon as we know it. In one sense this highlights the ways in which differences from Earth function in the films. In another way this falsity acts like the multiple presentations of the moon in *Le Voyage*: what camp does is bring forth an unknowable moon, but an unknowable moon which is still the moon, just a camp one.

Part 3: Almost There

Chapter 7

Destination Moon (1950)

[Transitions] It is strange that so much theater takes place in a film which is mainly known for its strive toward realism. *Destination Moon* (1950), directed by Irving Pichel and produced by George Pal, is often credited with being the first "'modern' science fiction film"[142] because it "includes a number of realistic details that combine to convey a very believable picture of future space travel"[143] which is due to the fact that "the director and producers enlisted the aid of top physicists to ensure that what they finally committed to film was as authentic as possible."[144] It tells the story of a number of astronauts who generate interest and financing for a mission to the moon mainly to prove that it can be done rather than with any kind of scientific goal in mind—or put otherwise, all the science was concentrated on the ground, just as Vivian Sobchack argues in contrasting the film with Christian Nyby's anti-scientific film *The Thing from Another World* (1951).[145] In *Destination Moon,* despite a number of technical setbacks all the astronauts return safely. In the discussion of camp films one of the arguments was that amid all the silliness the moon actually began to poke through. In this part, the opposite operation will take precedence. In other words, the elements of camp that slip through all of the supposed fidelity will be our best lunar guides. This can be seen in the first lunar presentation that takes place in the film, which happens in the first seconds, before the opening credits.

While this initial image of the moon is meant to be realistic, what is theatrical about its presence is the way that it is "revealed": there is a cross dissolve from right to left revealing the light side of the moon first and then leaving the dark half empty. Orchestral music plays as the camera slowly zooms in.

Then the dissolve is reversed, from right to left, leaving the screen black. This moment is theatrical because the technique for revealing the moon is foregrounded, much like the sinking stage set of the lunar surface in *Le Voyage* when the earth was sighted. The cross-dissolve in *Destination Moon* presents the moon as if theater curtains are drawn and then closed. This foregrounding of technique takes place repeatedly throughout the film. It is significant because techniques of transition are actually one of the main presentations of the moon in this film, being at least on par with the direct lunar images shown. Yet at the same time what is strange about this opening shot is that it implies that the moon will be central to the film, although this is hardly the case: *Destination Moon* seems to do as much as it can to ignore the moon altogether, which might be the reason for so much theatrical lunar presentation when it does appear.

Another cross-dissolve is used during the journey between the earth and the moon. There is a dissolve from left to right, just as with the moon at the beginning of the film, but this time the object revealed is the earth. Then there is an odd dissolve, where the rocket on which the astronauts are traveling to the moon is seen traveling through space. However, because of its placement, it momentarily seems to be flying *through* the dark portion of the earth. Then the earth fades out and the rocket ship is seen flying through space on its own before, in another dissolve, the moon fades in and the ship seems to be flying into the light side of the moon. Then, at the end of this sequence, the ship fades out and the moon is left on its own. Then the crew aboard the rocket fades in and is momentarily seen together with the moon and stars.

These types of transitions are commonplace and perhaps it is a classic case of over-interpretation to be looking at them. However, they seem to deserve critical attention as they also take place on the approach to the moon and when taking off from the moon to go back home.

But what do these transitions entail? Grouping a number of different types of imagery here—that of rocket in earth, rocket in moon, moon and astronauts—indicates that there is a common feature underlying them all. One common element is a term already mentioned in this chapter: theatricality.

[Theatricality] The term "theatricality" is used here in order to distinguish between theater as a place and theatricality as an event. As Samuel Weber argues in *Theatricality as Medium*, theatricality is more and more identified with "spectacle," meaning a privileging of action over place, or of "energy over matter, of force over bodies, of power over place."[146] In these scenes from *Destination Moon* the energy of the transitions (theatricality) is being read instead of just the content of the imagery (place, theater). At the beginning of the film theatricality took place in the unveiling and then veiling of the earth. In the shots here it is seen in a technique of horizontality; through these dissolves a number of elements are presented together when they should not be in reality. Thus the rocket is seen flying through the dark side of the moon or the moon appears in the middle of the rocket ship. In this sense, the qualities of the moon and rocket, such as "solidity" and "opaqueness" are put in question; like in camp, these qualities are slippery, or, as Harman describes horizontality, "the qualities of a thing break off from the thing as a whole and seem partially distinct from it for the first time."[147] However, this technique is not limited to this movie, nor does it have some particular connection to representing the moon. In fact, such a gathering (of different elements together) and a breaking-off (of the qualities of the rocket and moon) is a common feature of dissolves, as filmmaker Germaine Dulac states in an article from 1924: "The dissolve is a means of moving from one image to the next in such a way that the end of the first is superimposed on the beginning of the next. It is also a technique with a psychological meaning. The images that are linked are related to each other so that the movement from one to the other is not jarring. The dissolve brings people and things together into a brief or lengthy whole."[148] Yet what is discussed below is less a psychology of the dissolve than looking at its relation to movement. The use of these additive and subtractive dissolves in the representation of the earth and moon together, or of the astronauts or rockets with either, indicate not only a connection or continuum between the separate objects being brought together by this technique but also a *piercing* of one in the other, resulting in a breaking-off of the qualities from an object.

[Continuous Transition] These descriptions of some of the transitions in *Destination Moon* aim at foregrounding a continuum between elements which are usually seen as being separate from each other. Henri Bergson's thought on *durée* has often been used to describe a similar function of cinema, although at the end of *Creative Evolution* from 1907 he specifically comes out against cinema in his attack on the intellect. My argument is that although Bergson's thought on duration will help approach what is happening in the film it is actually his criticism of cinema which is most "lunar."

At the beginning of *Creative Evolution* Bergson recapitulates his concept of *durée*. The main idea is that we usually perceive existence as passing from "state to state," such as from warm to cold or from watching a film to not watching a film.[149] However, existence is actually a duration rather than a succession of separate states: "there is no essential difference between passing from one state to another and persisting in the same state... the transition is *continuous*."[150] The continuity that Bergson proposes replaces the illusion of the ego which is created to tie all of the supposed blocks of experience together. Instead of a stable ego which makes sense of experience Bergson proposes a foundation of change: "for a conscious being, to exist is to change, to change is to mature, to mature is to go on creating oneself endlessly."[151]

Elements of both the blocks that Bergson detests and the continuum that he proposes can be found in the transition images from *Destination Moon*. First, the blocks are not only found in the individual frames that make up celluloid cinema but also in the elements which are combined, for example the moon and rocket ship. At the same time these elements are shown not to follow one another but rather to transpose into one another, or for one to run on into the other. This can be seen in the placement of one image inside the other, such as the rocket that appears in the dark side of the moon or within the earth. Because of their aesthetic resonance these dissolves are not just about the passing of time, meaning an indication of elided time during the space journey, but they also indicate a thinking of the two elements together which then foregrounds the duration of the dissolve. These new combined images are the product of the "evolution" part of Bergson's *Creative Evolution,* for out of continuous transition change arises: "duration means invention, the creation of forms, the continual elaboration of the absolutely new."[152]

One of the main figures in bringing Bergson into the purview of film studies is Gilles Deleuze, who begins his *Cinema 1* with a short chapter entitled "Theses on Movement: First Commentary on Bergson." His main point is to show the illusion of finding cinematic movement outside of images themselves, just as Bergson showed the illusion of the ego. While Deleuze states, as we did above, the cliché that "Cinema, in fact, works with two complementary givens: instantaneous sections which are called images; and a movement or a time which is impersonal, uniform, abstract, invisible, or imperceptible, which is 'in' the apparatus, and 'with' which the images are made to pass consecutively,"[153] he wants to show how images themselves can be *movement-images* or *time-images*. Regarding the movement-image, what Deleuze means is an image which shows movement itself, such as a crane shot from King Vidor's *The Crowd* (1928). This shot is a movement-image because it shows the movement of the camera which in one sense goes beyond that of the individual images shown.[154] Thus in Bergsonian terms it is not that there are images and then movement applied to them but rather that the images themselves have a duration. As John Mullarkey argues, for Deleuze "*Image is everything... everything is in motion.*"[155]

But what then of Bergson's critique of the cinema? At the end of *Creative Evolution,* in preparation for a re-evaluation of some aspects of Greek philosophy, Bergson claims that the mechanism of "ordinary knowledge" is like a film projector in that understanding is forced upon what are seen as a number of concrete states rather than trying to "attach ourselves to the inner becoming of things...."[156] Yet it is here that Deleuze brings out a key aspect of Bergson's thought: for Deleuze "becoming" is to be found in images themselves rather than the cinematic apparatus. At the same time Deleuze separates himself from Bergson by showing how cinematic images actually have a privileged place in such a discussion.

But what about the transitions in *Destination Moon*? Change is not found in a single image, such as was found in the accelerated moon above. Instead a different mechanism is in place: one image seems to go *through* another. A rocket appears *in* the moon or the earth; the moon appears *in* the rocket command module. Thus movement is located not in the image but rather in the image in the image. This doubling is a different kind of togetherness in which the separate blocks of celluloid cinema are not just brought together in Eisensteinian montage but one image *pierces* the other. Of course this piercing is something which is seen everyday outside of film. For example, think of seeing a car from the side: there are a number of seemingly discrete elements involved, such as doors and windows and side panels. But at the same time there are images which pierce each other: the interior of the car is seen through the window; parts of the axle are seen through the hubcap; a light bulb is encased in its plastic housing.

What the transitions in *Destination Moon* do is foreground the way that filmic images are continua in the way that a single shot is always a composition of lighting, acting, movement, props and so on, which at least since Christian Metz has been irreducible to a single element.[157] These dissolves help make this horizontal continuum of the togetherness of the image visible. However, the dissolve is not the only way this foregrounding takes place in the film; another technique is seeing things upside-down.

[Upside-Down] As *Nude on the Moon* offered nudity as one, if not the only, indication that action was taking place on the moon, in *Destination Moon* being upside-down is seen as an indication of not-being-on-Earth. For example, when the astronauts are on their way to the moon they are amazed at seeing the earth from space. In the first scene where the astronauts are seen observing the earth one of them appears from the top of the screen. The position of the astronaut is due to the fact that they have been floating around the command module of the rocket in the micro-gravity of their celestial environment. This non-Earth location is denoted quite simply—by one or more of the astronauts appearing on an unexpected side of the frame. A few moments after this scene some of the astronauts exit the rocket to free an antenna that has frozen over; again, the trope of being upside-down is used to convey a sense of being away from home.

But there is something more going on here than just being upside-down. In this shot the astronauts are looking away from Earth and in the direction of the moon, but they never comment upon seeing it. Instead, one says "Take a look behind you" and they all turn away from the moon to look, once again, at the earth. Thus the moon gets short-changed in this moment of illustrating what it is like to be in space, which is merely to be inverted. But at the same time seeing things from a strange point of view has a rich history in moon films. It was best seen in the anchored location of the rocket passengers in *Frau im Mond*. Here nothing different is being developed: what space does is make one's locus apparent, at least for those not used to going into space. This making-visible took place through an interplay between subject and object in previous films; here it takes place by turning the camera on its head.

[Trash] But what happens to the moon in this equation? Why is it being ignored? I argue that it is because *Destination Moon* is actually not a "moon film" at all. In fact, it treats the moon like trash. The film focuses on the possibility of traveling to the moon and back rather than on any experience of being on it. For example, early on in the film the astronauts are looking for financial backing to build their lunar rocket. In order to inform and interest investors they have commissioned a film explaining the science behind a moon landing. The form this film takes is a Woody Woodpecker cartoon.[158] When Woody arrives on the moon he never even leaves the rocket: his first question after landing is how to get back to Earth, which he does immediately after poking his head out the rocket door, which he does just to make a snide comment rather than to take in the marvel of the lunar surface. In a similar manner, when the astronauts actually land on the moon they never leave sight of their ship and shortly after landing are informed that they used too much fuel during their problematic arrival; therefore they have to lighten their load as much as possible before attempting a return flight. This prompts not only dismantling as much of the ship as possible but also removing keys from pockets and even considering leaving one of the crew members behind. Thus instead of exploring the moon or foregrounding how different it is from Earth (one astronaut does get one bounce in, but is immediately told to stop clowning around) the astronauts dump much of the contents of their rocket, turning their part of the moon into a trash heap before leaving back for Earth as soon as possible.

In this sense *Destination Moon* is a film about "trashing" the moon by showing how the moon itself is not particularly important. This was also seen in the Bergsonian transitions in which it was not the elements that were important but rather the piercing of one in the other. However, this notion of trashing does not apply to all of the elements in the film, for it is the earth which holds a privileged position rather than the moon. In fact, in deference to scientific accuracy, the landing site on the moon was chosen by the director because of its sight of Earth: "Robert Heinlein, the author of 'Rocketship Galileo', on which the movie was rather loosely based, had selected the crater Aristarchus for the landing site, but Bonestell did not like Aristarchus. Rather, he opted for the crater Harpaulus, at a high northern latitude, facing the Earth, so that the Earth would appear near the horizon where the camera would capture it along with the lunar landscape." [159] In this sense being on the moon is all about Earth.

Chapter 8

Countdown (1968)

[Summary] While *Destination Moon* is a moon film which is actually about the earth, *Countdown* (1968), Robert Altman's third film, is a moon film which is about cinema. It tells part of the story of the space race between the Americans and the Soviets during the cold war. The Americans have learned that the Soviets are landing on the moon so they devise a crash program to land one astronaut on the surface first where a supply module has been previously placed. There are no scientific experiments attached to the mission. The astronaut is just meant to be the first to land on the moon, get to the supply module, and wait for up to a year for NASA to finish the Apollo program and bring him back. Originally astronaut Chiz (Robert Duvall) is supposed to make the trip. However, he is a colonel and since the Soviets are sending civilians on their mission it is decided that the Americans must do the same; thus civilian Lee (James Caan) goes in his place. Most of the film centers on the preparation for the flight, and the relationships between the astronauts and their wives. Once Lee is in space he needs to locate the supply module before he can land. He does not see it from the rocket but decides to land anyway, causing much worry as he traverses the surface and exhausts almost all his air before finally locating the module. The film is not particularly engaging and most critics have approached it through the lens of whether it reflects some aspects of the later work of the *autour* director. While Robert Kolker claims that "*Countdown* is a studio film and gives no idea of what Altman was to do,"[160] the fact is that he was fired from the film shortly before its completion because of the producers being unable to comprehend a very key element of Altman's style: overlapping dialogue.[161] Other attempts by Altman to make the film more personal, including having Lee run out of air before finding the supply module at the end of the film, were scrapped.[162] Thus perhaps the film should not be so easily dismissed from the Altman canon.

[Blackboard] Just as with *Le Voyage*, the first lunar image on the film is found on a blackboard. However, while the moon in Méliès' film was fuzzy and needed to be filled in with scientific knowledge, the blackboard moon of *Countdown* is thoroughly known, for the image is a detailed photograph; this lunar mission is not about increasing the understanding of the moon, but about reaching its surface before the Soviets during the cold war.

The image on the blackboard illustrates the flight plan for the Pilgrim I mission which has been quickly put together. The "figure 8" drawn around the moon on the blackboard indicates the pass the astronaut will make over the moon looking for the survival module beacon. If the beacon is not found then the landing is supposed to be aborted, although later one of the scientists says that the reason a human is in control of the rocket is to make an emotional decision and land no matter what.

At the same time the "scientific" position of this and other lunar imagery in the film takes on a different function than that of *Le Voyage* and other films. Instead of having the learned discussion of the scientists bolster the validity of a lunar mission, now it is the technicality of the imagery that lends weight to the scientists' plan. There are numerous scenes in which information about the moon flight is being presented with the main support for the accuracy of this information being the image placed behind the speakers. Thus "speaking in front of the moon" shows that such representations are acting as a support for what is being said. This does not necessarily mean that they illustrate what they are talking about but rather that they act as a placeholder for the knowledge, expertise and previous work done by the scientists of NASA. In other words, exploration is over. The moon is understood. Although there is much debate about the logistics and safety of the mission there is no discussion about lunar knowledge per se, just about how to get there.

[Reduction] These images of the moon are images full of detail. However, they are also paradoxically images of reduction in the sense that the moon is taken out of the sphere of wonder as it becomes a background to the drama, which is about beating the Soviets. Thus, although the moon appears in highly accurate images and sketches, its function is reduced to a finish line rather than an object which yet escapes our full understanding, as it of course will forever remain (along with every other object).

This reduction is seen in a more literal sense in the flip-side of these detailed images when the lunar landscape is reduced to pitch dark. During his mere 3-weeks of training for the moon landing Lee practices a number of procedures in a simulator. What is interesting here is that there is no attempt at all to approximate the appearance of the lunar surface. There is light representing sunlight or earthshine, a model of the supply module and a harness which hooks onto the astronaut to simulate the low gravity of the moon. But otherwise the exercises take place in total darkness. In this manner the moon is reduced to nothing.

As a counter-argument it may seem like the moon contains at least two elements here: a buoyancy caused by the lower gravity of the moon (simulated by the harness) and a specific and intense light (simulated by the large lamps). However, both of these elements are negated once Lee reaches the moon. There is virtually no light on the lunar surface and when Lee does traverse the landscape there is almost no buoyancy whatsoever, at least when compared to the manner in which he leaps around the training facility. In addition, most of the shots of the moonscape are devoid of striking features, except for emptiness.

The images of the lunar surface are in stark contrast to the representations of the moon presented behind the scientists waging an information war. They are also quite different from the light and relatively feature-filled picture of the moon Lee gets while flying overhead, searching for the beacon from the supply module. These differences seem to indicate that there is something about being *on* the moon which reduces what can be said about it. However, rather than being an instance of films like *Destination Moon,* which are less about the moon than they seem, perhaps this is an instance in which the moon actually becomes *cinematic* in that, in the words of Alain Badiou, "A film operates through what it withdraws from the visible."[163]

[Badiou] This quotation from Badiou is taken from the beginning of his chapter on film from *The Handbook of Inaesthetics*. For Badiou, inaesthetics are a means by which philosophy functions as a "submission" to the dictums of art rather than the other way around.[164] The inaesthetics of cinema lie in the way that the visible passes by and is always a part of the past, which is due to the separation and disappearance of individual frames on the move: "Cutting is more essential than presence—not only through the effect of editing, but already, from the start, both by framing and by the controlled purge of the visible."[165] In other words, in cinema everything you see goes away. The philosophical submission to this going-away is a thinking of what Badiou terms *the event*, be it May 1968, a scientific discovery or falling in love. For Badiou one of the definitions of an event is that it took place in the past: "I will term situations in which at least one evental site occurs *historical.*" The reason that being historical is essential for an event to take place is that localizing something in history "is subtracted from representation" in that it is not a part of the bustle of the present but it is something that needs to be reconstructed. It is in the possible antagonisms between reconstructions and the event reconstructed that truth becomes possible.[166] This antagonism has been seen a number of times in the moon films when gaps have opened between objects, their presentations and observers; in other words, this is a vertical tension. However, Badiou also locates this tension, or what he calls the "impurity" of cinema, in how the art of cinema is always at odds with its complicity in capitalist consumption.[167] Yet, as Jacques Rancière argues, Badiou's thesis on cinema needs to be radicalized. Cinema is not just impure because it challenges representation by being subtracted from it (because it is in the past), rather cinema *impurifies* the other arts it contains (painting, acting, lighting and so on) by being subtracted from them;[168] this is more of a horizontal position. In this way the difference between the scientific moon used during press conferences and the bare moon on the surface can be understood in terms of reduction in that the moon is presented and then removed from that presentation. This is where the inaesthetics of the moon lie. In other words, the elements that are removed from the presentation of the moon while Lee is on its surface, such as light and reduced gravity, do not foreground what we know about the moon because they are gone; the truth of the moon is to be found elsewhere, and that is in the procedure of reduction itself.

[Love] There is another element of reduction in the movie, but it has nothing to do with presenting the moon; instead it has to do with presenting love. For Badiou, there are only four kinds of events that matter: art, science, politics and love.[169] Love can cause a "postevental" truth to exist in the world when it becomes a universal address. It becomes a universal address when a subject is "faithful" to a historical event site: "when the subject as thought accords with the grace of the event—this is subjectivation (faith, conviction)—he, who was dead, returns to the place of life. […] He recovers the living unity of thinking and doing. This recovery turns life itself into a universal law. […] This is what [Saint] Paul calls love."[170] What this "according" entails is a declaration of love, for what declaring love does is "to move on from the event-encounter to embark on a construction of truth."[171] Usually this declaration comes in the form of saying "I love you," which can of course be an empty manipulative phrase but which can also be a kind of promise. The addresser of this phrase, according to Badiou, has the chance to say "I shall extract something else from what was mere chance. I'm going to extract something that will endure, something that will persist; a commitment, a fidelity. And here I am using the word 'fidelity' within my own philosophical jargon, stripped of its usual connotations. It means precisely that transition from random encounter to a construction that is resilient, as if it had been necessary."[172] Thus love can be an event because it arises out of a past randomness, where and when love arises cannot be predicted. But following up on this love, accepting its consequences and keeping faith to its disruption, is what Badiou means by "fidelity." But there is another way to be faithful to the love-event without saying "I love you." There is something that cinema and Badiou's thought on cinema adds to this discussion which makes such fidelity, despite not being about the moon per se, moon-like. This addition is a moment of reduction, or restraint.

In *Countdown* there are two moments which lead to a discussion of "reduced" or "restrained" loving between astronaut Lee and his wife Mickey. The first is seen before Lee is assigned to the spaceflight and Chiz still believes he is going. Chiz and another astronaut are having dinner at Mickey and Lee's house and Chiz is explaining the mission. After everyone goes home Mickey and Lee are in bed together, still wearing their dinner clothes and talking about how tough it will be for Chiz's wife Barbara to handle her husband being on the moon for up to a year while waiting for the Apollo mission to be ready to pick him up. Lee, speaking of Barbara, says "She's a tough babe," to which Mickey responds, "Yeah, well we're all tough." Then Lee lightly flicks Mickey's behind, which is shown in close-up. The gesture of the flick could of course be interpreted and responded to in many different ways by Mickey, the least offensive of which being something along the lines of Lee suggesting that she is being cheeky. However, Mickey responds by taking her husband's hand. In other words, in this scene Mickey expresses concern about Barbara; this moment is interrupted by Lee's flick, then Mickey again expresses concern, but this time for Lee, or maybe for them both as a couple, because being sent into space is always an option for an astronaut, even if she thinks this time it is happening to Barbara and Chiz. This is a gesture of fidelity because a moment of concern is broken and then returned to again. This is a moment of historicity because the current gesture of concern (say, for Lee) not only relates to the past gesture of concern (for Barbara) but also to all of the times that Mickey has already had to be tough. This is a moment of love because the gesture of fidelity involves more than one person, thus it is of what Badiou calls "the Two scene."[173] In a sense it is also an image of restraint, in the sense that Lee is "restrained" from going to the moon (by Chiz going), which opens a space for tenderness to occur. Restraint can also be seen the next time Mickey and Lee are shown together in bed.

At this point Mickey and Lee know that Lee is going to the moon instead of Chiz. The scene takes place in a hotel room before the launch. Mickey is upset because reporters hound her everywhere. She says she tried to see Lee at the training facility but was denied access. Then she asks if he can spend the night. He says, "No, not all night" and there is a dissolve to a shot of the moon rocket on its launch pad. It is night. While watching this scene my assumption was that the dissolve indicated sex. However, the next shot shows them lying on the made bed fully clothed. Thus my assumption changes to that they did not have sex. Instead they spent the time talking. And for the first time Lee drops his tough-guy attitude and opens up about being scared to go up into space and about his fears of spending so long in the lunar module waiting for the next astronauts to arrive. Like the scene of holding hands this is another moment of intimacy brought about through something not happening, this time sex. This is the idea of restraint: if something expected does not happen then opportunity for something else to take place comes forth. This is also the basic idea of potentiality, from Aristotle and Avicenna onward. In addition, it also suggests the idea of the masochistic passivity of Shaviro's visual fascination. The reason that a gesture of restraint is important is because it represents a moment where "anything" could have happened; it is an event. In one sense when images of the moon are similarly "restrained," meaning minimalist or barren, in the film there is the possibility for something unknown to occur. This "unknown" is seen in challenges faced during the training simulations or the dangers of actually surviving on the moon. When the "full" moon is shown in illustrations there is no such room for doubt or danger. Thus the reduction of the moon is the moon, at least at its most fantastic.

Chapter 9

2001: A Space Odyssey (1968)

[Title] Stanley Kubrick's *2001: A Space Odyssey* (1968) is generally considered a movie which "deconstructs the myths of the final frontier"[174] and "epitomized the awe and grandeur of man's ascent to the stars."[175] In short, "The film is now generally acknowledged as a great masterpiece of modernism...."[176] However, the film slots into the moon discussions presented here as a conservative piece of kitsch with a single moment of interest. The kitsch element is easy, for any film that begins with a half hour of watching actors messing around in monkey suits falls prey to this moniker. However, locating the interesting aspect of the film takes up the bulk of this chapter. The film concerns itself with the appearances of a monolith. It painstakingly tries to imbue the black box with a sense of ambiguity. The opening act places the monolith at the crux of humanity's evolution away from other animals. Another time it is found buried in the moon. At the end of the film an astronaut travels inside it and finds a fetus. The main issue with this film is the way in which it posits the monolith as the source of change. Other moon films, made after the 1969 landing (like *Apollo 18*), posit a more challenging mechanism for change in that change actually comes about without an object, or without a cause, instead resulting from chance and randomness.

The first shot of *2001* provides a combination of elements that has not been seen until now: while the sun is seen "rising" from behind the earth, as it was observed in *Frau im Mond,* this sequence in Kubrick's film is seen from over the horizon of the moon rather than from inside a rocket ship (the moon is hard to see, but it lies at the bottom of the screen).

The discussion of *Frau im Mond* focused on how seeing the

sunrise away from the surface of the earth localized the position of the viewer. In other words, seeing a familiar event from an unfamiliar position foregrounded the location of the seeing, both on Earth and in space. This was seen to have two consequences: first it opens a gap between the subject and the object and second, by localizing the point of view in a body, it was seen that thought is dependent on embodiment, which was then used to suggest how a world that existed before bodies also existed before, and thus outside, thought. But what effect does this scenario from *2001* have? The relationship between the sun and the earth is the same. What is different is the point of view from which this relationship is seen. At this point in the film there is no one on the moon with whom to match this point of view (although later in the film the moon is shown as having been colonized). Thus it seems that the beginning of the film suggests that there is something about the moon itself which could localize a point of view in this way. But then as the shot progresses the moon fades out and the title of the movie takes its place. The title of the film is not superimposed on the moon but replaces it. Thus, in the context of the discussion of the moon here, the film places itself in the position of a localizer. The film makes some claim at being able to make relationships that have been taken for granted visible again, as was done with the earthrise in previous films. However, despite its great effort in this direction the film fails at this task in a number of ways. Mainly it is because the mysterious monolith is not nearly mysterious enough.

[Tools] *2001* is divided into four parts. The first, The Dawn of Man, shows some early hominids who learn how to use tools once the monolith appears in front of them. The tool they use is a bone and in the final shots of this scene one hominid is shown throwing it into the air. A match cut then "turns" the bone into a space ship, showing both the similarity in toolness between the two objects and the role that learning to use tools had in the intervening three-million-year evolution of our species; in other words, an object, a bone, which has been encountered in daily life by the hominids, has taken on a new function by becoming a tool for killing. This is perhaps the most famous shot in the film. The question this sequence poses is how an object "taken for granted" can be seen in a "new enough" light to take on another purpose. One way to approach this topic is through Heidegger's thought on "tool-being," which has been revised and expanded by Graham Harman in a book of the same name.

Heidegger indicates that things are encountered as a part of a world rather then being individuated objects: "These 'things' never show themselves initially by themselves, in order then to fill out a room as a sum of real things."[177] A well-known example that he gives of a thing that begins to become individuated is a hammer, albeit a broken one. For example, when we use this tool "correctly" then we experience its "handiness" (*Zuhandenheit*),[178] meaning its average everyday position in the world which does not give rise to thought. When a tool is broken we then begin to experience a kind of "objective presence": "When we discover its unusability, the thing becomes conspicuous. *Conspicuousness* presents the thing at hand in a certain unhandiness."[179] This is a kind of vertical understanding. In a parallel argument it was said above that when the location for a point of view becomes unusual, or "broken," such as with the rocket passengers in *Frau im Mond*, then what has been taken for granted starts to become visible, and thus we experience the location rather than just being caught up in its everyday use.

However, in *Tool-Being* Harman explores an unthought element in this equation when he aims to foreground the manner in which a hammer is experienced as being more than "merely" a hammer even in its everyday state. In a similar argument to the role of "gathering" within the fourfold, this "mere" [*bloß*] gathers both the handy hammer and the unhandy one. Harman ties the concept of the mere to the presence of the gap between multiple representations and their object (indirectness) and thus the objects themselves become problematic (horizontality), which leads to him calling his kind of philosophy "object-oriented": "The idea of an object-oriented philosophy is the idea of an ontology that would retain the structure of Heidegger's fundamental dualism, but would develop it to the point where concrete entities again become a central philosophical problem."[180] The most obvious example of the moon not being "merely" a moon was seen in the multiple representations of *Le Voyage* and in the way that truths of the moon leaked out of its camp presentations.

In the tool scene from The Dawn of Man section of *2001* there is an explicit representation of the idea of the broken tool: a bone is transformed from its everyday handiness as part of a skeleton, which has been come across countless times by the early hominids, to a multi-practical tool which allows this group of hominids to dominate others and thus evolve into us. The film also posits an engine for the "mere" in the film: the reason that the bone is seen as not merely a bone is because of the monolith. This is seen when early hominids are chased away from their watering hole by a rival group. They spend the night cowering under a ledge and wake up in the morning to find the monolith having strangely appeared. Then one finds a bone and uses it to kill the rival group's leader. Then the bone is tossed in the air and shown to be connected to the orbiting spacecraft.

However, there is another striking image of the monolith taking on the function of the *mere*: during the appearance of the monolith among the early hominids its position as the *mere* is foregrounded in a shot where it appears with the sun and the moon. In the opening shot of the film the sun was seen to "rise" above the earth from the vantage point of the moon. Here the sun is seen rising above the top edge of the monolith with the moon appearing above it. Thus the position of the earth in the first shot is taken over by the monolith in this one. It was argued previously that the relation of the sun and earth is taken for granted, or is *handy*, when the sunrise is seen from Earth. However, when the same event is seen from the rocket ship in *Frau im Mond* this handiness is destabilized, or revealed as unhandiness. This change was brought about by the localization of a point of view. In the opening of *2001* it is argued that this unhandiness was brought about by some kind of experience of the moon, or perhaps by the movie itself. In this image it seems as if the monolith is being posited as the locus of this change. Thus in one sense the monolith turns the *mere* into a concrete problem by embodying it, making it both visible and ambiguous.

Yet, by placing the monolith in the position of the instigator of this change a too easy approach is given; for even if the "reason" for evolution is unknown or ambiguous the monolith still acts as a placeholder for such a key to understanding to take place; in other words, it does not matter that the reason for learning how to turn the tool into a bone is unknown because the monolith represents the possibility of knowing such a reason. This argument is bolstered by the fact that Kubrick has said he does not want to offer any kind of simple explanation for the monolith, for it would ruin the movie.[181] However there is very little difference between saying that there is a single answer for what the monolith is and there is a single answer for what the monolith is but this answer is withheld—although in Arthur C. Clarke's short story "The Sentinel," which was the basis for *2001* and which takes place entirely on the moon, a simple answer is given, the monolith is a sentinel put on the moon by aliens for "watching over all worlds with the promise of life."[182] The way that Kubrick seemingly removes the clear reason for the monolith to exist is problematic, although not because a mechanism for change is posited. There is a mechanism for this tool-change to take place, however, this mechanism is not unknown but is rather the unknown. This is a fundamentally radical notion of the "mere" and it is a concept developed by Quentin Meillassoux in the published extracts of his PhD thesis,

The Divine Inexistence.

[Randomness] Meillassoux argues that our planet has experienced three fundamental changes in its existence so far: the creation of something out of nothing, the creation of life out of matter and the rise of human thought out of animal intelligence.[183] This leads him to argue that another change could (or not) take place and that because each new state has not been contained in the other (meaning that something is not contained in nothing, or that life is not contained in non-life)[184] we cannot not know what state might arise after the next big shift.[185] These moments of change are due to randomness since there is no telling what the next change might bring. Meillassoux uses this idea to develop his theory of ethics, which might be briefly encapsulated thus: because death cuts off any chance to right wrongs the only fundamental ethical position to take is that of the simultaneous resurrection of everyone who has ever lived followed by their perpetual state of being. Because we do not know what the next big change will bring (or if it will come at all) one thing it could (but not necessarily) bring about is this vision of perpetual resurrection. Meillassoux then goes on to posit that although we cannot state that God has ever existed it is now possible to believe in a God who does not exist as yet, since the existence of a God is also a possible outcome of a random moment of change.[186] This is the power of the randomness of Meillassoux's argument, for "if immanentism is maintained in fully radical form, it implies a world with nothing outside that could limit its power of novelty."[187] In other words, "If advent is immanent, then it is absurd; thus it is capable of anything."[188]

Meillassoux is discussing the same moment of change that is depicted in the bone scene in *2001*. The difference is that Kubrick posits a source for this change, which is the monolith, which for all its ambiguity is at least known to be something from another world. For Meillassoux nothing is posited as the instigator for change except randomness. If we are to truly live in what can in brief be called a "meaningless" universe then we really must always be prepared for another large random event to take place at any time and for no reason.[189] This is the heart of the practical ethics of his immanentism. And despite this reading of *2001*, Meillassoux denotes science fiction as a privileged location for a visualization of such randomness. While on the one hand "science fiction is fiction inside the space of science. Inside the space of science you have to think disorder, hazard, as something which is a disorder inside an order, inside a continuity,"[190] it is also a place in which a world could be imagined "where there is some order, but the scale of disorder is too large for science, too disconnected for science," where things just disappear or a Newtonian world turns into an Einsteinian one.[191] Here randomness could occur because there would be experience (such as of a black monolith) but logical consequences of such experience would play no part (the monolith could do something not logically connected to a monolith). This would be a "world where you have this continuity, and inside it you have this pure break."[192] The monolith in the tool scene does not present such a break because its cause of disruption is too clear. However, a scene on the moon posits a notion of change closer to Meillassoux's reading. It comes in the form of a noise.[193]

[Earth] The second "noisy" monolith is found on the moon. One of the main features of the moon in *2001* is of course the earth. Although the film features many realistic looking shots of the moon upon the approach of Dr Floyd (William Sylvester), who has been sent there to investigate the appearance of the monolith, a large proportion of the shots taking place above and on the lunar surface include an image of Earth in the background, including the landing, two astronauts already on the planet watching the landing, flying across the lunar surface in a moon car and during the scene which will occupy us shortly, when a group of astronauts go examine the monolith which was dug up under the surface. What this series shows is something quite simple: in order for the moon to be defined it must be defined in relation to the earth. In other words, without the earth the moon could not be known. Or, as Bill Anders, astronaut on the Apollo 8 mission, has said, "We came all this way to explore the moon, and the most important thing is that we discovered the earth."[194] Thus Earth has a normalizing function: it tames the potential strangeness and ambiguity of being on the moon; or, if we see Earth in the sky, we know we are on the moon. This normalization was already challenged in *The Cosmic Voyage* when the cosmonauts landed on the far side of the moon and found themselves bereft of this comforting lodestone. In contradistinction, the almost-constant presence of the earth during the external lunar shots in *2001* reflects the same relationship between the earth and the monolith pointed out at the beginning of this chapter in relation to the opening credits: both the hominids' monolith and the monolith on the moon have the function of normalization because the earth normalizes the moon just as the monolith normalizes the randomness of change, at least as Meillassoux might read it. However, this smooth dialectical relationship is disturbed by a sonic presence.

[Sound on the Moon] In the second part of *2001*, entitled TMA-1,[195] Dr Floyd has traveled to the moon because of a strange report of a found object. The moon base has been sealed off from all outside contact because the object is supposed to be of extraterrestrial origin and the manner in which the public should be informed is strictly controlled. Dr Floyd travels to the archaeological site where the monolith has been found. Once again, in order for strangeness to take place on the moon the astronauts need to go deep into the ground, a feature seen from *Le Voyage* onward, although the earth is still seen out of a corner. After a brief examination of the monolith the astronauts pose in front of it for a photograph. It is during this moment that a loud piercing sound causes the astronauts to grab their helmets as if trying to cover their ears. They seem to be in pain. It is the end of this part of the film.

The sound that the monolith seems to emit should be inaudible because there is no air on the moon; thus the sound is already strange because it should not be happening. But the sound becomes even stranger because there is not any cinematic proof that it is coming from the monolith, for there is no physical sign of the sound being emitted. What takes place instead is similar to what Michel Chion calls the *acousmêtre*, a term he takes from early avant-garde musician Pierre Schaeffer and which he defines as a separation between a sound and its source. This effect can be seen, for example, in the voice of "mother" in Alfred Hitchcock's *Psycho* (1960): there is an ambiguity in the film as to what is the origin of the voice and once it is matched to Anthony Perkins' body the mystery of the film is solved.

For Chion, the *acousmêtre* is interesting in *2001* in relation to HAL's voice; this is not because we do not know where the voice is coming from but rather that HAL's personality is totally contained in his voice, since there is just "circuitry" behind it. Thus in the scene where Dave shuts HAL off,[196] the loss of voice turns into a loss of subjectivity. What is interesting to us here is the way in which Chion describes this moment of loss, which he says "is an inscrutable and unthinkable moment which we can comprehend only by what goes before and after. There is no gradual transition from one to the other."[197] The first part of this description is similar to Badiou's reading of the event in that the moment of the event is unknowable, however, truth is to be found in the fidelity one shows to this unknown afterward; in the second part of the quote Chion sounds like Meillassoux in the latter's description of change in that there is no "half-life" that exists between matter and life but rather there is just the spontaneous and abrupt eruption of life where there was no life before.

For Chion this event of change takes place in the moment of the loss of HAL's voice and also the moment when the unattached voice of the *acousmêtre* becomes tied to a subject.

In the scene of the monolith buried in the moon from *2001* this unknowability can be seen in the connection between the screech that the astronauts hear and the monolith itself.[198] It is in this unknowable moment that randomness comes forth. This is the moment of the "mere" in Harman's description, in that the sounds show that the monolith is not merely inanimate. What is more, the moment that this sound takes place is one of the few in which the earth is nowhere in sight. In fact, after the sound is heard the camera zooms in on the astronauts cutting off any chance of a reassuring earthly presence. This is a real moment of ambiguity in Kubrick's film, one of the rare ones. It prompts Chion to make the rather wild suggestion that "as this event happens to occur while they are getting ready to photograph the monolith, for all we know the monolith is emitting its electro-magnetic screech in protest against being captured on film."[199] A slightly more sober reading is that in this unknowable moment, a truth of the moon comes forth: the moon can never be matched to the presentations at hand, no matter how ambiguous or alien their form. This statement only becomes clearer when the surface of the moon is reached for real.

Part 4: Close-Up

Chapter 10

Moonwalk One (1970)

[Summary] As mentioned above, one of the most similar texts to *Shooting the Moon* is Jalufka and Koeberl's essay "Moonstruck," which focuses on the accuracy of moon representations in films. It has been cited a number of times already. However, the authors end their essay at the Apollo 11 moon landing. Their last filmic example is *2001*, which "easily 'wins'"[200] in its realistic depiction of lunar travel and exploration.

One of their main bones of contention with the realism of science fiction films taking place on the moon is a simple one: the moon is depicted as jagged and rough rather than smooth, something all filmmakers from Méliès onward could have known by looking through a telescope.[201] However, when we turn our attention to the actual moon footage it is surprising how some of the fictional lunar tropes that have been previously developed are found in film shot on the lunar surface. For example, the moon is still fuzzy, accelerated and there are images of rockets blending into the surface of the moon as they pass over, just as seen in *Frau im Mond*. In one sense this should not come as a surprise because all recorded images will share certain aesthetic features which are tied to the medium with which they are taken. But this also points to ways in which these ontological features of the moon are more realistic than previously suggested. A number of essays have recently come out following a similar line of thought, and work within the emerging field of New Aesthetics will be key for a number of aspects of this chapter.

The images taken by the Apollo 11 crew are initially examined through the lens of Theo Kamecke's documentary *Moonwalk One*, finished in 1969 and released a year later. The film made a brief appearance in cinemas at the time but was quickly forgotten, only to be re-released in 2007 when interest in the Apollo 11 landing was heating up for its 40th anniversary. Although Kamecke was given access to NASA footage of Apollo missions, he adds his own mystical element to the film, most noticeably by opening and closing it with images of Stonehenge. However, similar to how unrealistic or camp elements of lunar representations were seen, at times, to foreground truths of the moon, here mysterious, fantastic and hard-to-read elements will be found in the actual moon footage itself, along with the contexts of its presentation.

[Pictures] However, before looking at *Moonwalk One,* there are two images from early Soviet and American missions to the moon which seem as if they had been culled from one of the fictional films under discussion. One is the first image of the far side of the moon, taken by the Soviet Luna 3 spacecraft launched in 1959 (images from space had been taken since 1946, when a V-2 missile was launched to take pictures of Earth from afar). The Luna 3 pictures were taken with special 35mm film which was developed on board, scanned and then transmitted back to Earth at either a slow rate when the spacecraft was at a close distance or a faster and less reliable rate from farther away. A total of 29 pictures were returned.[202] Because of this process of production and transmission the images are of a rather low quality, although this low quality adds an aesthetic dimension of its own; these images of the far-side of the moon are definitely fuzzy (Figure 11).

The idea of a fuzzy moon was first developed in connection with the moon appearing on the blackboard in the astronomers' hall in *Le Voyage*. There it was argued that while the earth featured a number of graphic devices which indicated a scientific knowledge which encircled it, the moon was a fuzzy ball resistant to such knowledge. Thus the mission to land on the lunar surface was meant to "fill in" the lack of knowledge about

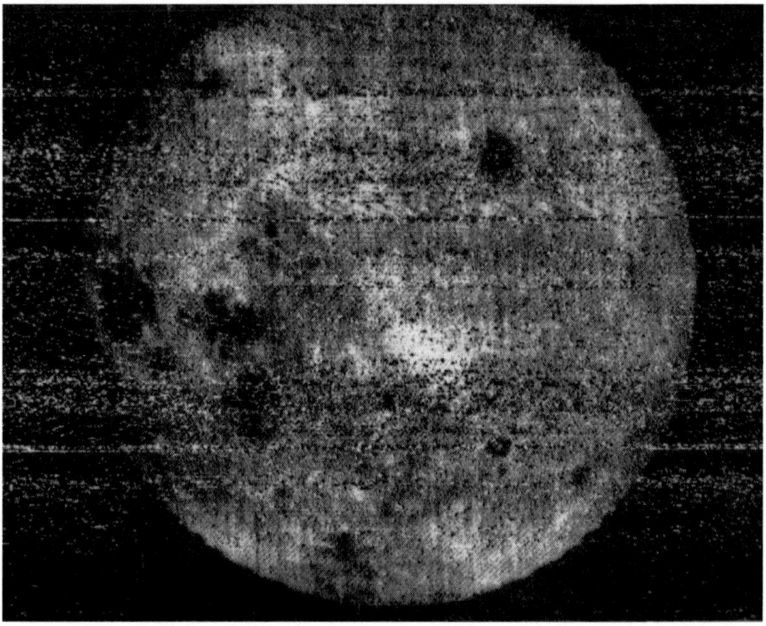

Figure 11. Far side of the moon taken by the Lunar 3 spacecraft. With permission from NASA.

the moon, which of course it did not, at least in a scientific sense. In the Luna 3 image of Figure 11 a similar vertical fuzziness is present, although it appears within an actual photograph of the moon and not within the realm of fantasy. On the one hand the image shows a side of the moon that had never been seen before; on the other, the image is difficult to read because of the interference of noise during its transmission process. This fuzziness indicates that photographing the moon does not equal knowing it, but only approaching it through the technology of the time, just as we do now. Therefore, although this photograph is a powerful record of the scientific progress of humanity it also shows that some lunar truth always lies elsewhere than in actuality. From another angle it can be said that *Le Voyage* captured a truth of the moon as it was seen by Luna 3: its fuzziness, even when seen from "up close."

Seven years later the American spacecraft Lunar Orbiter 3 took another kind of photographic first: it produced the first image of a human-made object on the moon, which it took from orbit. This happened when it photographed the unmanned American Surveyor 1 lunar lander (Figure 12).

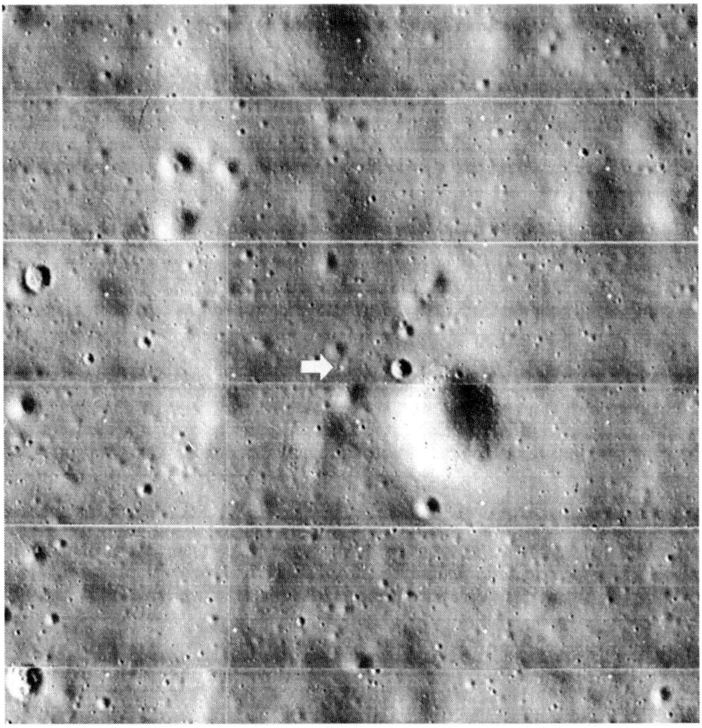

Figure 12. Surveyor 1 lunar lander photographed by the Lunar Orbiter 3. With permission from NASA.

Surveyor 1 had landed on the moon in June of 1966 and transmitted over 11,000 photographs to Earth. The Orbiter image is interesting for this study because Surveyor is very difficult to distinguish from the natural features of the moon surface due to the quality of the photograph (its position is indicated by the arrow), just like the rocket in *Frau im Mond*.

The rocket traveling above the lunar surface in Lang's film

was used in a discussion of Benjamin Noys' reading of acceleration, meaning speeding up the laws of a system in order to destroy that same system. In the context of *Frau im Mond* this was interpreted as the rocket speeding up to match the speed of the moon and then "disappearing" into it. But is a similar thing happening here? In one sense the image of Surveyor 1 points to the weakness of the political agenda of acceleration, for there is no guarantee that acceleration will lead to anything positive rather than just barbaric. In the context of this image this means that the Surveyor craft just disappears, rather than enacting any kind of change to a lunar understanding. However, as Shaviro argues in his reading of acceleration and cinema, although acceleration might not make political sense it makes aesthetic sense, since the importance of acceleration is for a difference to remain, no matter how slight, of the accelerated object and the system it finds itself in, which in our case is the rocket in the surface of the moon. "This is not easy," says Shaviro, "since there is always a risk that the work will get lost within the spaces that it endeavors to survey, and that it will become yet another instance of the processes that it is trying to describe."[203]

At first it seems that the lunar lander succumbs to the "risk" of acceleration that Shaviro points out, for once on the ground the lunar lander disappears into the surface, meaning that to the lay eye it is almost impossible to detect among the other landscape features of the moon.[204] Some of the reasons for this disappearance include the high level of contrast between dark and light elements of the landscape, the fact that the image is taken from so far away and the appearance of the lander as a round object in the midst of so much other roundness. However, perhaps this is the wrong approach. In fact it is incredible that the lander is visible at all from such a height. In other words, the reason that such a relatively small object can be picked out from the ground at all is because images of the surface before and after the landing can be compared, and differences noticed. Thus

Surveyor does not succumb to this risk, and a view of acceleration which is reversed from what was seen in *Frau im Mond* is developed, for in that film the rocket sped up to the velocity of the moon and was lost in it: there were no other images of the surface to which to compare it. With Surveyor 1 difference remains, but only when reconstructed later. This is the same configuration of Badiou's event.

[Take-Off] Returning to Kamecke's documentary *Moonwalk One*, an initial observation of the film is that it puts its mystical cards on the table right away by opening with shots of Stonehenge and a voice over intoning "Stones from afar brought by man to this place where no stone stood before."[205] However, the film includes a wide array of footage from NASA engineering cameras and moving images shot on the lunar surface which makes it an important stepping stone for this discussion of actual footage shot on the moon. Kamecke tracked down footage from a multitude of cameras that NASA had used to record potential failures during launch. He says: "I was reading one of NASA's launch manuals in preparation and found that NASA had 240 engineering cameras around the launch pad capturing everything in slow motion... Once they shot it, it was bundled up and sent down to Huntsville, Alabama for analysing, if they didn't use it, it got thrown in a box and left to rot. Luckily I was able to dig it out and then use it in the film. It was certainly better than the limited three media spots NASA was giving out to the Media."[206] The reason that this footage is of interest here is that it contains images of objects taken by objects without human aesthetic intention. This will place the footage under the emerging field of New Aesthetics, which has been (roughly) tied to Speculative Materialism on a number of occasions.

During the take-off sequence two main types of images are shown: those showing the release mechanism of the launch pad and those showing close-ups of the result of the great heat and force exerted by the rocket engines. These are easily some of the most wonderful images taken in relation to (but not of) the moon, and the reason is that they are the unplanned products of industrial engineering (a similar image is seen in Figure 13).[207]

Figure 13. Apollo 11 liftoff. With permission from NASA.

When we cross the threshold of the first feature film with a one-billion-dollar production cost I can only hope that the excessive budget is due to setting up real events to be recorded in a relatively unplanned manner by a plethora of cameras in order to obtain, by chance, interesting images. This is part of the strategy of New Aesthetics, which is simply "the incidental visual residue of the performance or enactment of a process."[208] In other words, as it was put in an article on the making of *Moonwalk One* appearing a few years after the movie's release, "One very ironic conclusion that Kamecke came to in considering NASA's type of filming was that it was pure Warhol."[209]

[New Aesthetics] Encouraged by a Tumblr set up by James Bridle in May 2011, the New Aesthetics movement has turned into a loose collection of artists, thinkers and engineers who are interested in aesthetic experiences produced by machines. These experiences can include glitch art, CCTV images, industrial videos and the culture surrounding drones. After a panel on the topic at the 2012 South by Southwest conference science fiction author Bruce Sterling wrote an extended piece for his blog hosted by *Wired* magazine in which he argues for the need to reinscribe a human component into the understanding of the appreciation of these images.[210] One of the approaches to the human understanding of such "visual residue" has been through trying to apply the work of Harman, Meillassoux and other Speculative Materialists to the topic, usually without much rigorous intent. For example, in the "Manifesto for a Theory of the 'New Aesthetic'" Curt Cloninger takes Sterling's critique to heart when he says that "'Things' don't affectively suss New Aesthetic images. Only humans 'get' NA images. There is no machine 'aesthetic', no robotic 'vision'. Humans invent aesthetic theories regarding the interpretation of machine-generated images. Machines do not invent aesthetic theories regarding the interpretation of circuit-generated images."[211] However, the manner in which Cloninger releases Harman from fulfilling the role of providing a theory for New Aesthetics is instructive.

In a section of his manifesto Cloninger discharges a number of philosophers from the canon of New Aesthetics. His treatment of Harman's reading of Heidegger is worth quoting in full:

> On to **Heidegger**: Graham Harman interprets Heidegger's *Vorhandenheit* (presence-at-hand) as an eruption of the thing out of its normal function in the world (its normal function is *zuhandenheit*, 'readiness-to-hand'). The thing was *there* all along; but we never saw it *this way* until now. This eruption is a useful way of understanding NA images. NA images are visual eruptions of everyday functioning systems in the world, systems humans never saw *in this way* until now. Like Heidegger's broken hammer—the carpenter only stops to reflect on it once it stops working as expected.
>
> New Aesthetic visuals don't necessarily 'reveal' a hidden 'truth'. It's not as if readiness-to-hand is false and presence-at-hand is true, or vice versa. They are just two simultaneous ways of being in the world. (Heidegger's genius—his 'sleight of hand'—was to draw our attention to readiness-to-hand without turning it into presence-at-hand.)[212]

Cloninger believes that Harman says that true things are there "all along" and it only takes one to properly "see" a thing in order to understand the truth that it has always been. This would be Harman's "horizontal" reading of tool being. Cloninger then says that in fact when things are seen properly they do not divulge a truth, rather they are just seen differently, and both ways of seeing an object are equally valid. This then seems closer to Harman's "horizontality," although Cloninger seems to reserve this position for NA only..

In other words, in the previous chapter on Kubrick's *2001*, tool-being was used to help understand the use of the monolith in relation to the early hominids' development of tools. The Heidegger of *Being and Time* was quoted as saying "When we discover its unusability, the thing becomes conspicuous. *Conspicuousness* presents the thing at hand in a certain unhandiness." This seems to support Cloninger's horizontal reading of how things are "always already" in a state of truth and they merely need to be unveiled by proper use, meaning using something "broken" because then its ontological properties come to the surface. However, letting Heidegger continue on from this quote we see that he explicitly makes this position horizontal: "But this implies that what is unusable just lies there, it shows itself as a thing of use which has this or that appearance and which is also objectively present with this or that outward appearance in handiness... This objective presence of what is unusable still does not lack all handiness whatsoever; the useful thing *thus* objectively present is still not a thing which just occurs somewhere."[213] For Heidegger this means that things which are present, at-hand, or unbroken still contain a measure of uneasiness. Therefore when Cloninger states that both handiness and unhandiness exist simultaneously and that one state is not truer than another he is actually reading Heidegger close to the way that Harman does. This is why Harman latches on to the use of the "mere" in Heidegger, as delineated in the previous chapter: objects which are present are not "merely" present, there is something which remains removed from the "use" we make of them.[214]

The reason that these arguments are being given space here is because Harman's foregrounding of certain horizontal aspects of Heidegger can then be rescheduled into a potential theoretical basis for New Aesthetics. Near the beginning of *Tool-Being* Harman locates Heidegger's thought on the broken tool as a place in which presence itself is strange: "The goal of Martin Heidegger's career was to identify and to attack the notion of reality as something present-at-hand. And although his proposed alternative to *Vorhandenheit* remains underdeveloped in his writings, it is in no way vague—that which first resists any reduction to presence is tool-being, performing its dynamic effect amidst the cosmos, always partly withdrawn from anything that might be said about it."[215] We have already come across the withdrawn aspects of things in relation to both indirectness and experience. What ties Harman's thought to New Aesthetics is the manner in which he redirects this withdrawnness away from *use* and locates it in the objects themselves: "contemporary philosophy needs to part company with Heidegger in the most radical way: *objects themselves* are already more than present-at-hand. The interplay of dust and cinder blocks and shafts of sunlight is haunted by the drama of presence and withdrawal no less than are language or lurid human moods."[216] Here lies the importance of the various launch images from *Moonwalk One*. It is not that they present a kind of aesthetics that are new or somehow removed from human observation, it is rather that the images show a horizontal tension between each other which indicates an independence from human thought. This is not because they were separate from human thought in space or time, but rather in possibility: a camera recording from within the heat blast of a rocket engine, bringing back images from this inhospitable place, are similar to the Luna 3 cameras taking pictures of the far side of the moon. It is not that the images themselves contain a truth, rather they show that human experience is not the limit of truth, and thus that there is an experience outside of that of humanity.

[T.V.] Neil Armstrong's first steps on the moon were taken on July 20, 1969, and were transmitted using the Westinghouse Apollo Lunar Television Camera which was mounted on the exterior of the landing module and then detached for use on the lunar surface.

The images transmitted to Earth by this camera also have something in common with previous images of the moon seen in a number of feature films: when seen by viewers on TV they were fuzzy and have very little relationship to any kind of visual "truth" of the moon.[217] By this I do not mean to imply that they are somehow false images but rather that they are examples of images which are more about absence than presence. For example, the difference of an image of Armstrong just before he stepped on the moon and that of Armstrong having stepped on the moon are quite wonderful in their expression of how little of a difference there actually is between them: they are both prime examples of fuzziness and little difference can be found between them.

"Stepping" on the moon is indicated by a figure standing up slightly straighter and a small gap opening up between that figure and the ladder. In this sense these images of the moon do nothing to fill in the fuzziness of lunar knowledge. In fact, tens of thousands of images had already been taken by unmanned spacecraft which had landed on the moon surface. Instead these images of Armstrong are on the side of experience, of documentation, and in this sense the "what" of what they record is of little value; value instead lies in the *theatricality* of the event, and in this manner these images have much in common with a number of images found in *Destination Moon* where, by citing the work of Samuel Weber, it was seen that action was privileged over space in that the spectacle of the moment was more important than providing a clear image of what was taking place. In other words, the images are "more than they show" in that they are not about what they present but rather about what is taking place at the moment.

[Close-Up] There is another type of lunar presentation in *Moonwalk One* and it has not been seen before. When the astronauts of Apollo 11 returned to Earth they brought back 22 kilograms of samples. This is an aspect of lunar missions missing from the films discussed so far, and it even proved an incisive plot point in *Nude* for all moon samples and pictures were left on the surface, thus putting the whole trip into doubt. In *Moonwalk One* the examination of the samples are given a relatively thorough treatment. One of the most interesting images is that of a minuscule lunar sample which is then put under a high-powered microscope, finding another lunar surface in its tiny structure. These images look like underground caverns of the moon, although this time they take place within microscopic lunar imagery rather than in digging out fantasy from under the moon surface.

Instead of "merely" indicating to what extent the lunar surface is being studied and understood during modern times, these images also show how much of that surface remains "beyond" what we can see and know, although the same techniques of extreme close-ups and unusual scales can have a similar effect on everyday objects, as Shaviro has shown.[218] In this sense these images, which are "actual" images of the moon, are beacons for how much continually remains hidden from view and thus separate from the world of human understanding.

Chapter 11

From the Earth to the Moon (1998)

[First Step] The sixth episode of the 1998 HBO mini-series *From the Earth to the Moon*, produced by Michael Bostick, Tom Hanks, Ron Howard and Brian Grazer, reenacts the Apollo 11 mission and is entitled "Mare Tranquilitatis," which is the name of the site where Neil Armstrong and Buzz Aldrin walked on the moon. Most of the episode is taken up with the human drama surrounding preparing for the mission, with only the last fourth of the episode devoted to the lunar journey. Although a number of shots from the actual footage of the mission are reenacted I will focus on the first steps made on the moon since they offer an interesting mix of actual and reenacted footage.

The shots that make up the first step on the moon from this episode proceed as follows:

1 – Reenactment. Neil Armstrong (Tony Goldwyn) descending the ladder of the lunar module.
2 – Actual footage within reenactment. Actual footage of Armstrong descending the ladder shown on a screen in the reenacted NASA mission control center (MCC).
3 – Actual footage of Armstrong descending the ladder shown on its own, but matched with that shown in the NASA MCC.
4 – Reenactment of the NASA MCC. The actual footage of 3 matches the eye-line of the head flight controller.
5 and 6 – The reenactment of Armstrong descending the ladder is matched with the eye-line of Buzz Aldrin (Bryan Cranston) waiting inside the lander.
7 and 8 – Again actual footage is shown of Armstrong descending the ladder which is matched with the eye-line of a reenacted flight controller who is praying during this

moment just before the first step on the moon is attempted.
9 – Reenactment of Armstrong hopping down from the ladder onto one of the landing pads of the lander and then hopping back up on the ladder to make sure the astronauts can get back inside.
10 – Reenactment of the first step on the moon. This is a close-up shot of Armstrong's foot as he touches the surface and makes his famous statement of "One small step for man...." (although he was originally meant to say "a man").
11 – The actual footage of Armstrong already having stepped on the moon is shown on a screen in the reenacted NASA MCC.
12 – The actual footage shown in the MCC is matched with the eye-line of the head flight controller.

This sequence is being given so much space here because it delineates four strategies for bringing the actual footage and the reenactments together. The first is found in 2 and 11 when the actual footage is located within a reenactment; in these shots the actual *fits within* fantasy. The second strategy is seen in 3-4 and 7-8 when the actual footage is allowed to take up the whole screen but is then matched with the eye-line of a character in the reenactment; here the actual footage is *matched with* fantasy. Numbers 5-7 provide a special case. Number 5 shows a reenactment of Armstrong descending the ladder while Number 7 shows the actual footage of the same event; this means that fantasy is *replaced by* the actual footage in this sequence. However, this reading is complicated by 6, which shows Aldrin watching, rather forlornly, Armstrong from inside the lander. The question that is addressed below is why this shot is necessary in order for the *replacement* found in 5 and 7 to take place. The short answer is that it foregrounds the presence of reenacted footage within the actual footage, thus attempting to reinscribe an element of authenticity into the reenactment. The last strategy can be seen in the shots presenting Armstrong's first step on the moon, in 9-11. While this first step was presented as something difficult to discern in the previous chapter, here this lack of clarity is improved by the reenactment which, at this decisive moment, provides a close-up of Armstrong's foot making its first impression on the lunar surface. This act is then matched with the actual footage shown on the NASA MCC screen in 11; therefore the fuzzy footage is filled in and the actual shot is *mended by* fantasy. That the actual footage is not allowed to fill the screen but rather is situated within the fantasy of reenactment in 11 only bolsters the need that the actual footage has for clarification.

Four strategies have thus been culled from this sequence: actual footage is *fit within* fantasy; actual footage is *matched with* fantasy; fantasy is *replaced by* actual footage; and actual footage is *mended by* fantasy. We have already come across the number four in connection with Heidegger's *das Geviert*. With "this" fourfold Heidegger will be looked at again, but in a different context. Some of the more problematic aspects of his thought on technology will help bring forth the horizontal manner in which these strategies function together.

[Technē] It is often-quoted that for Heidegger "the essence of technology is by no means anything technological."[219] By this he means that the essence of technology is that it *reveals*: "Technology comes to presence in the realm where revealing and unconcealment take place, where *alētheia*, truth, happens."[220] However, at first it seems strange that Heidegger includes technology in revealing. Previously revealing was connected to unveiling a more profound experience of a thing, such as the broken hammer being a more truthful experience than everyday use of the tool allows. With technology it seems that this revealing is not so positive, for what technology does in its revealing is to *challenge* [*Herausfordern*], as in to pressure. With technology "a tract of land is challenged in the hauling out of coal and ore." This challenging then leads to revealing, as Heidegger continues: "The earth now reveals itself as a coal mining district, the soil as a mineral deposit."[221] Revealing is "negative" here in that technology is an *"enframing"* [*Ge-stell*] of nature[222] rather than the pre-industrial age fieldworker who would supposedly merely "set in order" the wild nature around them in a kind of balancing act.[223] Enframing is for Heidegger the name for the essence of technology: "Enframing means the way of revealing that holds sway in the essence of modern technology and that is itself nothing technological."[224]

The concept of enframing is reflected in different ways in the strategies of the "first step" scene *From the Earth to the Moon*. The first strategy of the actual footage *fitting within* the reenactment seems the closest at first. Numbers 2 and 11 showed the actual footage of Armstrong on the moon literally framed by the edges of the screen of the reenacted NASA MCC. Although this at first seems like a too literal translation of enframing, with the MCC screen "framing" the actual footage, what makes this analysis possible is the work that such enframing does in the shot. For Heidegger enframing is revealing in the sense of turning something natural into something useful, like a river into electrical power. Thus the actual footage here seems to be "natural" while the enframing instrumentalizes it, turning it into something to be usefully mined. But what is "natural" about a Westinghouse Apollo Lunar Television Camera recording astronauts in space suits descending the ladder of a lunar lander?

If "natural" is meant as what is *not* constructed by humans then the manner in which these images show what is *outside* of human construction is the manner in which the fuzzy and difficult-to-read shots of the first steps on the moon are always "more than they show." Interpreting this "more" takes up the bulk of the following chapter which reads a number of moments dedicated to exposing the moon landing as a hoax. However, these shots from *From the Earth to the Moon* instrumentalize the actual footage by bringing its "fuzziness" into the easy readability of the reenacted footage, which is in focus, in color, and the actions which take place in it are easy to discern. In other words, the actual footage is "challenged," in the Heideggerian sense, into becoming unnaturally readable. This is seen to an even greater extent in the way that the first step on the moon is clarified: in the actual footage seen in 9 and 10 the step was nearly invisible, in 10 and 11 this step is clarified or *mended by* the reenactment which shows it in close-up. Thus the reenactment "reveals" what lies veiled in the actual footage.

[Danger] However, one of the most interesting aspects of Heidegger's discussion is that he locates something positive within technological revealing, but it is located within its "negative" aspect. Enframing is ugly. It "blocks the shining-forth and holding sway of truth." Thus such an abuse of nature is dangerous for humanity: "where enframing reigns, there is *danger* in the highest sense."[225] However, Heidegger follows this statement with a quote from Hölderlin's poem "Patmos": "But where danger is, grows / The saving power also." In Heidegger's reading of the poem "to save" here means "to fetch something home into its essence, in order to bring the essence for the first time into its proper appearing."[226] While Heidegger does not flesh out the way danger lodges truth he does say that proper comportment is important: we see truth "provided that we, for our part, begin to pay heed to the essence of technology."[227] The problem is that this "taking heed" is a *linguistic* position for Heidegger: in order to see the truth in the danger of technology we need to question, to ask, to think.[228] However, instead of focusing on the linguistic element of this argument,[229] a more horizontal approach will be taken by locating this danger within objects themselves rather than the manner in which they are experienced.

In "Technology, Objects and Things in Heidegger" Harman first reiterates his theory regarding tool-being and then delineates Heidegger's take on technology through an earlier version of "The Question Concerning Technology," a lecture from 1949 entitled "Insight into What Is." The main contribution of the first section is the way in which Harman locates an independence from human givenness or thought not within the "broken tool" of what Heidegger calls presence-at-hand (something revealed, or *Vorhandenheit*) but rather in the everyday functioning tool of what Heidegger calls readiness-to-hand, or *Zuhandenheit*. This is because, in brief, while there must always be *someone* to experience the essence of something (Heidegger's linguistic dependence, as pointed out by Derrida), the fact that an everyday object in its most common form and use can "break" and become unusual, or conspicuous, indicates that there is an aspect of this everyday object itself that exists outside human understanding; this means that "the ready-to-hand must withdraw from the system of the world altogether—otherwise it could never malfunction. While this latter conclusion goes beyond Heidegger's own self-interpretation, it is the only way to make sense of the tool-analysis."[230] It is the location of something "beyond" human experience within everyday objects that allows Harman to develop Heidegger's thought along a horizontal reading of the location of "saving power" within the "danger" of technological revealing.

In the second part of his essay Harman examines the seemingly self-contradictory sequence that technology a) reveals, and is thus presence-at-hand; b) but is also something which instrumentalizes, and is thus something which is readiness-at-hand; and yet c) is something which allows for "saving power" to become present. This seemingly contradictory nature of technology happens because everyday objects themselves are removed from totalized understanding.[231] However, Harman argues that this reading is not contra Heidegger but rather following Heidegger's logic to its own end, for "Despite the horror of technology, Heidegger contends that we can see the lightning-flash of being in the essence of technology. By stripping everything down to such a miserable form of presence-at-hand, it confronts us with the call of distress from being itself."[232] The question then becomes whether a reading presents itself in this scene from *From the Earth to the Moon* in which the fantasy, or reenacted elements, contain truth in themselves rather than just being vertically contrasted with the more "profound" actual footage shot on the moon; this is what Colleen Boyle argues when she privileges the imagination as the only place in which to gather the fragmentary knowledge of the moon into any kind of whole.[233]

[Reenacting] There were four strategies found in the sequence presenting the first steps on the moon. It was argued that the first and last, namely having the actual footage *matched with* and *mended by* fantasy, were located within the negative aspect of technology in the sense of instrumentalization. But what about the other two strategies? They also involve both reenacted footage and actual footage. Is there a way in which, following Harman's reading of Heidegger, a "truth" can be found not within the ambiguity of the actual footage, as done in the previous chapter, but rather in the reenacted footage itself? In 3-4 and 7-8 a shot of actual footage was presented "full screen" and then matched to the eye-line of one of the reenacted NASA flight controllers watching the event on screen. Thus it was argued that actual footage was *matched with* fantastic footage. In 5-7 a reenacted Armstrong is seen descending the lander ladder, then a reenacted Aldrin is seen watching the event from inside the lander and finally actual footage of Armstrong descending the lander ladder is matched with the eye-line of the reenacted Aldrin. Thus it was argued that fantastic footage was *replaced by* actual footage, since the *mise-en-scène* of 5 (reenactment) is set up the same as 7 (actual). In both of these strategies the reenacted footage is being connected to the actual footage. In the *matched with* strategy this is simply done by treating the actual footage as being a part of the world of the reenactment. In the *replaced by* strategy this is done by having the reenacted footage of Armstrong's descent being retroactively legitimized by the actual footage of this descent.[234]

The connection between the two types of footage is not just found in the similarities of the formal compositions of the shots but also in the reenacted Aldrin "seeing" both the reenacted Armstrong and the actual Armstrong from the window of the lunar lander; thus the reenacted footage is being placed *on par* with the actual footage. In this way the two "types" of shot are not being seen as separate but rather as different aspects of the same. What allows this to happen is the *gathering* of these different types together. The main argument for the presence of such a gathering in lunar films was seen in the first chapter in a discussion of the fourfold in conjunction with indirectness and *Le Voyage*. The fourfold plays a large part of Heidegger's reading of technology, and Harman ends his essay by stating that "For Heidegger, the only way to think the essence of a thing is to recognize that things have a 'fourfold' structure. But this fourfold (*Geviert*, in German) is a thorny topic best discussed elsewhere,"[235] which Harman does, most clearly in his book *The Quadruple Object*. However, *From the Earth to the Moon* makes its own contribution to this area in that the final episode of the mini-series is, in part, a reenactment of the filming of *Le Voyage*, where the "strength" of the reenacted footage itself begins to come forth.

[Unfuzzy] The final episode of the *From the Earth to the Moon* mini-series is called "*Le Voyage dans la Lune*" and it intersperses reenacted and actual footage of the final manned mission to the moon, Apollo 17, with a reenactment of and actual footage from

Méliès' film. The episode was written by Tom Hanks who also stars as Méliès' assistant. The moon first appears in this episode in a series of cheap montages, at the beginning in which Hanks' voice-over attempts to connect the imagination expressed in Méliès' film with the courage to actually send astronauts to the moon.

The first time that the moon appears during the reenactment portion of the episode is the same as in Méliès' original film—it appears on a blackboard. However, while the moon was seen as "fuzzy" in Chapter 1 here it is quite defined: the unclear moon of Méliès' film comes into focus as a detailed drawing of the face in the moon which is soon to appear.

And it is here that a shot appears which does not in the original: a medium shot of Professor Babenfouillis (originally played by Méliès, here by Tchéky Karyo) explaining his plan to the other members of the astronomy club. The earth is represented by a number of geodesic lines which once again represent a certain level of scientific knowledge. The moon, however, is not fuzzy but false. It is clearly represented as the face in the moon, which might also be true for the image of the moon appearing in the original film (although it is relatively hard to make out). Thus in the reenactment what is being stressed is not the scientific knowledge to be gained from such a voyage but rather the courage it took to propose it in the first place. However, restricting the value of the original film in this manner is undone by the manner in which it is inter-cut with the reenactment.

[Matched Action] A relationship between the Apollo 17 mission and the reenactment of Méliès' film takes place through a strategy of *matching*. There are a number of moments in which the action of *Le Voyage* is inter-cut with real and reenacted action from Apollo 17. These cuts give an interpretive value to the older film. For example, gunpowder is set off to simulate the explosion of the moon rocket engines in *Le Voyage* and this is matched with the loud roar of actual footage of the Apollo 11 rocket taking off; a volcano is seen exploding in the reenactment of Méliès' film and then the reenacted Apollo 17 astronauts are seen finding orange soil on the moon, which is later shown to be evidence of volcanic activity; and in a link with perhaps the least interpretive value, the reenacted astronomers in Méliès' film are seen going to sleep immediately after arriving on the moon which is matched with Apollo 17 astronauts talking about their sleep patterns during their mission.

This matching strategy is meant to give *Le Voyage* a kind of "predictive power," which has long been seen as a false validation strategy when dealing with science fiction.[236] However, this is not all that this matching does. The presentational strategy of *matching* has already been seen in this chapter in connection with 3-4 and 7-8 in which actual footage of the Apollo 11 moon landing was matched with the eye-lines of NASA flight controllers in a reenacted MCC. This strategy was dismissed rather offhandedly above as representing the more "negative" aspect of technology in that the actual footage was instrumentalized by the reenactment. However, the situation is different here: both pieces of footage are reenactments. Thus it is the relation between the two which is foregrounded rather than what one "side" does to the other. This relation of matching could also be called *gathering*, since what is being stressed is the way one image relates to the other. Such gathering has popped up repeatedly in this discussion under the aegis of *das Geviert*. It should also be remembered that for Heidegger enframing is gathering, as he states in "The Question Concerning Technology": "Enframing is the gathering together...."[237] The reason that this gathering is seen as important is that it points to the "more than" of an object. This was seen in Harman's discussion of Heidegger's broken hammer. In a strange coincidence this final episode of *From the Earth to the Moon* also features an image of a hammer near the end, when Apollo 17 astronaut

Jack Schmitt (Tom Amandes) uses the last moments of air of the last astronaut to step on the moon to throw a geological hammer into the air.

[Moon Hammer] One of the last gestures performed by a human being on the moon was to throw a hammer into the air. An actual image of this feat was taken on the surface and was reenacted in this episode. In the discussion of *2001* it was argued that the throwing of the tool into the air was diminished in the Dawn of Man sequence by the interpretable presence of the monolith, a certainty which was destabilized by the noise that the Moon monolith made. Here the hammer on the moon takes on the quality of an ordinary object which is shown to be strange even in its non-conspicuous state: it turns into nothing other than what it is. This is because the hammer being thrown here is in no way broken; instead, in perhaps the most interesting moment foregrounded by this mini-series, the only thing that makes this object different is that it is on the moon.

Chapter 12

Was It Only a Paper Moon? (1997)

[The Unaskable] James Collier states in a voice-over that his documentary video *Was It Only a Paper Moon?* (1997) will "Ask the unaskable questions...." What he means by this is that he will question whether humans ever landed on the moon. However, he inadvertently asks a different kind of unaskable question during this introductory monologue. At this point he is defining for whom this film is made. He means to say that the video will challenge those who believe in the moon landings and will provide a "rational power of questioning" to support those who do not believe. However, Collier makes a mistake when posing the very first question of the video. He asks: "Do you assume man has landed on the moon? If your answer is 'no' then this video will surprise you." Supposedly he means "If your answer is 'yes'" but this is not what he says. This does not mean that Collier is "wrong" but rather that a mistake he made has remained in the "text," an event which takes place more than once in the video. For example, when describing the dimensions of a lunar landing module he says that the width of a doorway is 32 inches; then, after he finishes his description his voice comes back much louder than before, a clear sign that this has been recorded during a different session, and he says "I misspoke. The door is 16-inches wide...." Then later, in a taped discussion with his antagonist Frank Hughes, who was NASA's Chief of Space Flight Training for over 30 years, Collier says: "So you're saying hypergolic fuel does not create a black smoke at all." Collier then pauses the video and interjects in a voice over, "You were taking advantage of me there, Frank. You knew I meant red opaque smoke," once again correcting himself. In all cases mistakes are allowed to remain in the video, although it is unclear whether the first one was ever caught by the filmmaker.

In this sense Collier fulfills his own stylistic guidelines. Near the beginning of the video he apologizes in advance for the unprofessional nature of the footage he has included, an issue which he turns into a positive quality: "Roughness is the form that true investigations usually take." Later he states that he is not "looking for the slickness that professional image makers have taught us to believe is true." So what is true for Collier? Roughness, the unpolished and the lack of professionalism now associated with YouTube, Vimeo and other sites that host user-generated content. As François Bucher argues in "Subjects of the American Moon: From Studio as Reality to Reality as Studio," "Nowadays it is clear that LIVE is also a form subject to post-production: LIVE is a filter that can be applied to an image much like the way a fake patina is applied to a copper surface for an inverse effect."[238] In one sense this "live" style indicates the veracity of what is being seen, although of course it is only a style which can be manipulated. What generates this type of realism for Collier is making a mistake and backtracking—leaving the "wrong" footage in the final version in order show that what is being seen has not been reified into a "believable" object. But at the same time this theory is challenged in his video, for actual NASA footage is often given its own space in the film, meaning it is left to run on without any sort of commentary whatsoever, most noticeably for three-and-a-half minutes when Collier shows the end of a section of a NASA documentary on Apollo 11 and the beginning of another section on Apollo 12. Thus the "slickness" of the actual moon footage is left to speak for itself. What is interesting here is not really roughness or slickness but rather that both are allowed to appear together, just as Collier's mistakes are allowed to appear with his corrections.

[Rewinding] One strategy for asking an unaskable question is stuttering; on this point I take Collier at his word. If you ask an askable question you have to have language for it, but to ask an unaskable one you need language that you do not have. This brings us to Derrida's critique of Heidegger and "the question": how to ask a question "outside" of a linguistic givenness? Of course this is impossible. However, Collier has an interesting approach to the problem, for one way to represent this contradiction is to backtrack or stutter in language, to say something inappropriately, or badly; or as Samuel Beckett put it, for something to be "Ill Said." So Collier makes a mistake and corrects himself rather than editing it out. He derides slickness in favor of roughness. He says he will challenge those who accept the moon landing as a given but, at the very start of the film, he mistakenly says that those who do *not* accept this fact are those who will be challenged. His overall strategy is one of missing his target.

However, there seems to be a contradiction in these examples because *not* removing mistakes seems like a conscious decision by the filmmaker, while *letting* the actual footage run or making the initial gaff regarding those who assume the moon landings are true seem relatively unintentional. And yet it is again the appearance of both techniques together which make this film an interesting base on which to develop a strategy for reading lunar images in film. Similarly, when Meillassoux debates whether Mallarmé intentionally encoded his poem *Coup de dés* both with the number 707 and with other numbers beside 707, his answer is "exactly." For it is at this point of indeterminateness that a kind of hesitation or stuttering takes place: "for a 'hesitant' code is not the pure and simple absence of a code, but a hesitation between two options that are now equally likely."[239] This hesitation is important for Meillassoux because it could go either way, and is thus a representation of the radical indeterminateness of chance.[240] In Collier's film this strategy takes on a similar function. He wants the landing to be real. He continually asks for it to be proven to him. He wonders why no one threw a ball up in the air on the moon and recorded it, providing definite proof (he does not discuss Schmitt's hammer throw). He ultimately seems to be saying that the recorded evidence just does not offer enough proof of the event, although at times he lets footage run on and on without any kind of interrogation, thus letting the truth of the moon images speak for themselves without argument. This strategy of allowing two poles to coexist opens space for the landing to be true or not, which is why the title of his film takes the form of a question, which the structure of the film turns into one of the "unaskable" variety.

[Fuzzy Reading] Collier develops a strategy of close-reading which attempts to mine the lunar footage of every possible detail related to its veracity. He states that the "evidence is not huge or glaring, but it can be small and hidden and difficult to see." The first example of this detail-oriented reading is an examination of a photograph taken on the moon which is blown up in order to show a set of girders which are seemingly a part of the ceiling of the film studio in which the photo was taken. My point is not to prove whether or not such images were filmed on the moon; rather, *Paper Moon* is being used as a guide to developing reading strategies which are similar in structure to the way some of the earlier films were seen to philosophize. This first strategy is to render images "fuzzy" to the point that they can be filled in with fantasy. This can be done by blowing an image up, reducing the quality of its reproduction or changing the speed at which it passes by through either acceleration or deceleration. These are similar strategies that Laura Marks indicates are essential to a "haptic" cinema, discussed below,[241] and they are key techniques to the manner in which Collier reads the rest of the moon footage he puts forth.

[Rooster Tail] It is through a constant manipulation of the image that the key piece of evidence in Collier's argument is presented.

He claims that the "rooster tail" of dust produced by lunar rovers (like that seen in Figure 14) would form a continuous arc quite high in the air while the dust thrown by the rover wheels in the actual footage is low to the ground and seems to hit a "wall" of atmosphere, thus indicating that it was filmed on Earth.

Figure 14. Lunar rover. With permission from NASA.

The techniques used to uncover this effect are in line with Collier's use of the term "video" rather than "film" to describe his own work: the image of the rover and the rooster tail is *paused, shown in reverse* and *repeated*. The use of video by Collier is part of his strategy to debunk the footage transmitted live by the Apollo crews. This aspect of debunking is a part of the larger culture of the VCR in relation to television, as Anne Friedberg has described in her classic text "The End of Cinema: Multimedia and the Technological Change": "The VCR demolished the aura of live television and the broadcast event."[242] Friedberg credits this effect to the ability for a viewer to control time through pausing, rewinding and fast-fowarding, all techniques Collier makes extensive use of. Or, as Paul Virilio puts it, "The machine, the VCR, allows man to organize a time which is not his own, a *deferred time*, a time which is somewhere else—and to capture it."[243] This organization is what allows Collier the distance from which to question the original footage, and is part of the reason he continually refers to his documentary as a video instead of a film.

The question of the rooster tail is a key point for Collier because his foil—Hughes—states that the rooster tail caused by the rover that astronaut John Young was driving is definitive proof that astronauts were on the moon: the arc it makes could only be possible in a lower gravity than Earth's. In *Paper Moon* a continuous shot of the rover being driven on the moon is allowed to play on, uninterrupted by editing or commentary for over a minute. This is a presentation of evidence. Then Collier explains in a self-interview that the dust kicked up by the wheels should have made a smooth arc behind the vehicle rather than rising up in the air and being "stopped" by a wall of atmosphere. The physics of this issue are not under discussion here; rather, the techniques which Collier uses to make his point are.

After a few minutes of explanation Collier plays the whole clip of the rooster tail again, from the beginning. After the kicked-up dust is mentioned in the audio track of the footage the original sound drops out and Collier provides a voice-over directed at Hughes. Collier says that the rooster tail should have gone up much farther and made a smooth arc. When a wave is seen emanating from behind the wheels, Collier directs Hughes' attention to it, asking him directly "See that wave?" Then, when the clip ends he says, "So, let's take a look at this again" and he plays the whole one-minute clip over from the very beginning, although the first 30 seconds or so are never used in his argument because no rooster tail is produced during this time. During this run-through Collier's voice is heard, all the while propounding another argument that the rover was too big to have fit into the lunar lander. Then, when the rover approaches the camera, Collier again points out the dust waves made by its tires.

When the clip comes to the end these waves are shown again, but this time in reverse. The change in direction is not commented upon; Collier simply asks his viewers to "Watch again, it is very important." Then, halfway through the clip being reversed it is put into forward motion again so that the waves once more can be seen. The sequence continues with Collier's voice-over complaining that when he told Hughes about this proof, Hughes hung up on him. This theme of "rejection" can be seen throughout the film, including its very last shot which is of the face of a NASA museum curator who would not allow Collier a sufficient amount of time to make measurements of lunar vehicles.[244]

However, this is not the end of the analysis of this scene, for Collier pauses the footage with one of the waves hanging in the air and directly addresses Hughes again, saying "This was your proof [that the landing was real]. And this is my proof that it was taken on Earth." During the second statement the film is again put in motion and the sequence ends.

This is one of the strongest examples of a horizontal strategy in the film in that the qualities of an image (the arc of the rooster tail) are being used to foreground tension in the image (the NASA footage). What brings about this strategy is the invention of the VCR; for, as Friedberg claims, "The VCR treats films or videotapes as objects of knowledge to be explored, investigated, deconstructed as if they were events of the past to be studied."[245] This distance allows a single frame to become an object of contention and one of the reasons for the expansion of the field of film studies. However, if the proof were in any way definitive for both parties then there would be no need to make a video or for Collier to present any other proof whatsoever regarding his claims about the moon hoax. However, this is not enough for either party. This is because images are simply hard to read. In her essay on the intractability of the video made of the beating of Rodney King by LAPD officers in 1991, Avital Ronell says that when such video was shown on TV, repeatedly in the case of the King trial, "television showed a television without image." The inability of television to articulate itself was read by video and "a rhetoricity of televisual blindness emerged."[246] In this sense video acted as a subconscious for television, showing that "TV does not know what it knows."[247] Video, then, can be "TV's guide," showing "how to symbolize the wound that will not be shown."[248]

At the same time, Collier is a logical extension of the wound caused by video in the sense that, as Virilio argues in *The Information Bomb,* "the alleged conquest of space [is] nothing more than a mere conquest of *the image of space* for a world of TV viewers."[249] This conquest of the image is connected to the role of the VCR in that it puts time in the viewer's hands. As Siegfried Zielinksi puts it, "The continual flow of sounds and images that were the hallmark of traditional broadcasting, was interrupted and partially frozen over by the time machine. The continuum of the event was confronted by the discontinuity of its viewing."[250] What this timely technique does is point to the way in which Collier treats the moon footage as a text which deserves close reading. Such close readings had been usually reserved for the realm of text. What Collier does in his video is to incorporate the slow-reading of texts into his video-appropriated world.[251]

[Textual Analysis] The truth of every recorded image released by NASA is doubted by Collier. For him this means that the truth he seeks about the moon landings has to find un-filmed support. He finds this support in the form of texts. The first instances of this are passages pointed out by pencil from *Lost Moon* by Jim Lovell and Jeffery Kruger (1994), the book upon which the film *Apollo 13* (Ron Howard, 1995) was based. This textual object, written by

Apollo 13 commander Lovell together with science writer Kruger (the latter of which was ridiculed for a *Time* piece on the Higgs Boson particle which was shown to be wildly incorrect), [252] is the first testimony given credence in *Paper Moon*. It is given credence is a very direct way, however, by presenting the actual page on screen, with passages underlined and pointed-out by an on-screen pencil. Collier reads aloud the text that is shown, moving the camera down the page. Underlined passages are stressed by the movement of the writing implement.

While this textual technique is repeated, there are other ways that printed matter is used in the video. Diagrams are also brought in for support. One image of a space capsule is used to show how astronauts wearing their spacesuits could never have had room to enter or exit, while another is from a patent application for a suit to protect astronauts from radiation on the moon, something that Collier thinks would have been so damaging to the health of the travelers that it should have received much more attention in the lunar literature.[253] Despite the lack of any direct evidence of hoaxing produced by these images, the fact that both were "published" as printed matter is enough for Collier to use them as support, unlike the video documentation returned from the moon. In fact, even fictional texts seem to take on more weight that the moon footage, as Collier asks why astronauts did not, following the advice of Jules Verne, put reflectors on the moon for people to see from Earth (reflectors were actually put in place by Apollo 11, 14 and 15 and by the Russian Lunokhod 1 and 2 missions).

[Fantasy Combats Reality] The use of textual support for the disavowal of filmic evidence is not being used to discredit Collier. Nor do I mean to make an Ongian argument that Collier is somehow a product of the print medium and is resistant to the fluctuations of the digital age.[254] Instead what is highlighted is the manner in which Collier takes, at times, an indirect approach to lunar studies. He is approaching the moon by that-which-is-not-the-moon. Although he has the lunar footage in front of him he turns to texts and drawings to support his claims for lunar truth. In other words, he is using fantasy to combat reality. Or, as Slavoj Žižek makes the case for cinema in general, "insisting on a false mask brings us nearer to a true, authentic subjective position than throwing off the mask and displaying our 'true face.'"[255] The strategy of using fantasy to combat reality is used throughout the lunar films being looked at here for there are many times that known facts about the moon are discarded in order to present something closer to the moon than such facts can supply. This was seen in its strongest sense in the chapter on camp in which absurdities about the moon twisted lunar images so far away from what was known that what was "left" of the moon in them, whether acceleration or nudity, was seen as a kind of lunar truth in itself. In *From the Earth to the Moon* something similar took place. In that mini-series the relation between actual footage and reenactments was seen to develop the way that objects were not found in the "broken hammer" of Heidegger's presence-at-hand (*Vorhandenheit*) but rather in the everyday aspect of readiness-to-hand, or *Zuhandenheit*. In the context of *Paper Moon* Collier does not find truths about the moon in the presence-at-hand of the lunar footage but rather in the readiness-to-hand of the commentary surrounding the event. In other words, here the task is to turn the actual footage (presence-at-hand) into a reenactment (readiness-to-hand); thus the film is in a sense the "opposite" of *From the Earth to the Moon*. It is logical that one place to enact such a change is in fiction, i.e. the fiction of a hoax theory.

Part 5: After the Fact

Chapter 13

Space: 1999 (1975-7), *Manhattan* (1979)

[Democracy] While most of the previous films focused on ways of putting the moon on screen, what unites films made "after the fact" of the lunar landing is a tendency to foreground the way an understanding of the moon is constructed rather than the way the image of the moon itself is put on screen. In other words, images of the moon take center stage rather than an attempt to understand or experience the actual celestial body. Although this idea has also been an aspect of earlier moon films, from the fuzzy moon on the blackboard of *Le Voyage* to Collier's interest in the validity of footage actually shot on the moon in *Was it Only a Paper Moon?*, in these films the-moon-as-image becomes even more central. The main consequence of this strategy is that once the constructedness of understandings of the moon becomes an issue, so does the constructedness of understandings of the earth. The manners in which this takes place are various: foregrounding the relationships between Earth and the moon which are taken for granted (by knocking the moon out of Earth's orbit, for example), taking an interest in representations of the moon on Earth (a lunar diorama in a planetarium) and giving new meanings to old tropes established in moon films (the earth hanging in the lunar sky becomes a symbol of fear rather than home). What all of these strategies share is that they deal with images of the moon rather than the moon directly. The overall consequence of this approach is that the earth and the moon become equally strange. Levi Bryant, building on Harman's work, calls this equality a "democracy of objects" which indicates that "all entities are on equal ontological footing and that no entity, whether artificial or natural, symbolic or physical, possesses greater ontological dignity than other objects."[256] This simply means that an understanding of the moon should not be constructed by an understanding of the earth. The moon has its own ontological truths. It is, like every object, "an object for-itself that isn't an object for the gaze of a subject, representation, or a cultural discourse."[257] In the following chapters a number of films are given short readings in order to bring out this commonality of films made after the Apollo mission landings. The result of these readings is quite simple: the moon escapes the earth. Yet one question remains untouched: what becomes of the earth once the moon is gone?

[Breakaway] The presentation of an object escaping Earth-bound givenness is the explicit subject of *Space: 1999*, a British TV series created by Sylvia and Gerry Anderson and airing from 1975-8. This is especially true for its first episode, "Breakaway."

The moon has been turned into a toxic waste storage facility for the earth. In this sense the moon has been instrumentalized, in the Heideggerian sense described above, by the earth. In other words, the understanding of the moon is constructed by earthly experience: it is nothing but a dump site for the toxicity the earth creates. And soon a mystery develops: a number of moon workers are dying of unknown causes. The answer to why this is happening does not lie in any strangeness contained on the moon, but rather one brought from Earth: the deaths are caused by fluctuations in the magnetic field emanating from the trash. Eventually these fluctuations reach such an intensity that they cause an explosion which hurls the moon out of Earth's orbit. Thus the premise for the series begins: the moon flies through space like a rocket ship, carrying its inhabitants to new adventures each week.

The first effect of this breakaway is that the relationship between the earth and the moon becomes warped; in other words, the objects of Earth and Moon remain the same while the way they are connected to each other changes. These changes are represented in a number of different ways: one shot shows the earth above the surface of the moon, which is a common set up for these films, although now the moon is seen flying away from the earth as it escapes Earth's orbit. Shortly after this another new movement for the moon is shown when it is seen "rocketing" out into space after the explosion. Finally, the astronauts "on board" the moon want to see what is going on. They tap into some images taken by a satellite orbiting Mars. The image they see on the screen shows the moon passing by Mars at great speed while the earth stands still. In fact, from the viewpoint of the Mars satellite camera, the moon approaches the satellite's field of vision and exceeds it, similar to the shot of the moon exceeding the frame of the rocket porthole in *Cosmic Voyage*. Yet there is a difference here because in *Cosmic Voyage* this movement was caused by the rocket landing, while here it is caused by the movement of the moon itself.

What is being foregrounded in "Breakaway" is not any kind of strangeness found on the moon surface: in fact, any newness that the moon might contain has been usurped by the needs of Earth to store its toxic waste on its surface. The only way for the moon to exist as a "democratic" object—meaning one existing outside Earth's givenness—is to break away from it. Thus images of movement are essential. But what is the connection between foregrounding the coordinates between objects rather than objects themselves? Jacques Rancière provides an initial answer in his reading of the mechanics of Robert Bresson's *Au hasard Balthazar* (1966). He says that the images in the film "are not primarily manifestations of the properties of a certain technical medium, but operations: relations between a whole and parts; between a visibility and a power of signification and affect associated with it; between expectations and what happens to meet them."[258] The "visibility" that Rancière mentions is the representation of the object, which in this episode of *Space: 1999* takes the shape of a toxic moon. The "power of signification and affect" is the ability of the relationship between objects to create new meaning. What is unexpected in "Breakaway" is the movement of the moon in relation to the earth. It is this movement which represents a break from the earth and a move toward democracy.

[Talking on the Moon] In Woody Allen's *Manhattan* (1979) the moon only appears briefly, but when it does it is as an image of the moon rather than the moon itself. When Isaac Davis (Allen) and his friend's mistress Mary Wilkie (Diane Keaton) find themselves caught in the rain they duck into the Hayden Planetarium in Central Park West in New York City. It is the first time the two have spent any time together without the company of their partners. The respite from the weather allows them to express an attraction to each other which is quickly shut down when Isaac tells her that he thinks it is not such a good idea for them to see each other again. However, later in the movie they do have a romantic relationship, although it ends when Mary goes back to her previous partner.[259]

There are three shots with Isaac and Mary on the moon: entering the planetarium and walking past a scale model of the moon; walking along the surface of the moon with the earth hanging above; and walking along the surface of the moon with a large model of Saturn hanging behind them. This sequence is followed by shots of the couple in complete darkness and then talking together in front of a star field. The scene ends with a cut to Isaac and Mary's boyfriend driving down a freeway in New York City, a location which is jarringly different from the lunar world.

Yet it is the appearance of a photographer on the moon which brings the role of the moon as an image into play. According to the logic of most lunar films, as the photographer walks into the frame and takes a picture he should be photographing either the lunar landscape or the earth in the sky. Yet he is actually taking a picture in the direction of the camera. In this sense he is taking a picture of a camera taking a picture of the moon. In one sense the photographer shows us what we already know: for in order for any image of a camera to appear on the moon, from *Frau im Mond* to the hammer throw of Apollo 17's Jack Schmitt, there had to be another camera there to record it.

Thus in *Manhattan* the construction of the moon by the earth is put into question not only by the theatricality of the planetarium, but also by the photographer showing the viewer where the camera is, foregrounding the way the moon is constructed both on and by the earth. But the moon in *Manhattan* does more than this, for it is the place where, later in the film, Isaac says to Mary that he had the "impulse to throw you down on the lunar surface and commit interstellar perversion with you." Thus it is not just, as Douglas Brode suggests, that Isaac's and Mary's "blossoming love takes place amid images of intergalactic darkness; *the dead surfaces of the moon suggest the deadness, and the moon madness,* of their oncoming relationship,"[260] but rather that when the moon is seen as a constructed image, the constructedness of the image of the earth comes into focus too. This democracy of images allows for new relations between objects to take place. This is seen in how Isaac and Mary are both freer on the surface of the moon than on the surface of the earth: the ties that bind them in their everyday lives loosen and an affair develops. Just as the moon took on strange movements in *Space: 1999* when it escaped the influence of the earth, Allen has chosen a diorama of the lunar surface as the setting for the beginning of Isaac and Mary's strange relationship.

Chapter 14

Apollo 18 (2011)

[Space] In the two films looked at above an equality was discovered between objects. This led to a foregrounding of operations or relations between these objects which had the potential to create new meaning. In Gonzalo López-Gallego's *Apollo 18* (2011) a slightly different strategy is in place: instead of a democracy of objects there is a democracy of images; this is seen in a variety of film stocks and effects which are used to equalize different types of knowledge. The film fits into the "mock documentary" genre in that documentary styles are utilized within a fictional setting in order to challenge ways that truth is put on screen. However, the film has a slightly different aim than Jane Roscoe and Craig Hight allow for the genre in their three "degrees" of mockumentary: parody, critique and deconstruction.[261] Although mainly falling into the last category, in that it assumes "that audiences are capable of resolving between these levels of reading" the difference between fact and fiction and thus "actively engaging in a critique of documentary,"[262] the focus of *Apollo 18* lies in the way that different types of footage presented together equalize strategies for putting knowledge on film. The result of this equalization is another kind of democracy, a democracy of images, which allows for an openness to various strategies of truth-telling rather than searching for only one form of knowledge; the term given below for this kind of openness is "planetary."

López-Gallego's *Apollo 18* easily "wins" at being the most "speculative materialist" film discussed here. This is because the desolate, empty everyday (ready-at-hand) environment of the entire planet of the moon takes on a weird and threatening character. In this sense, "space" becomes an issue in that the terror of the film is not localized (it is everywhere).

While *space* in cinema is usually seen from a psychoanalytic, semiologic or perceptual perspective,[263] here the approach is philosophical; more specifically, a speculative materialist approach is taken in which the main concern is the experience of objects outside the closed circle of human thought.

Space is horizontal. It is the tension between the multiple ways we engage with an object, or between the multiple ways an object engages with other objects; in other words, space is the never-reachable totality of all the possible ways one object can engage with other objects, whether the object is a person, an apple, a rock, a character in a film or one piece of celluloid taped to another.

For example, I can look at an apple from above, below, from the side and I can cut it open and look at its inside; I can taste it, caramelize it or freeze it; the apple can fall from a tree, get squished by the hoof of a horse or get struck by lightning: however, the apple will always exceed all of these ways of engagement. The apple is always in excess because even if you put all of these approaches to the apple together they will never *become* the apple. Space is the tension engendered by this "never becoming" or "always exceeding." In the words of Harman, "Space is the duel between these sensual qualities and the mysterious real objects that signal from somewhere beneath them, often in cases of surprise and disruption."[264] In this sense the term *outer space* can be read literally, in that it is the existence of a real object outside the human frame of reference.

In other words, real objects can always surprise us because we can never exhaust their possibilities. This means that surprise is possible because of space. Or, without space, nothing new would arise.

While this is a relatively new emphasis in philosophy and cinematic thinking (starting with a conference on speculative materialism in 2007), in science fiction criticism taking the tension between sensual qualities and real objects seriously has a rich history. For example, Mark Rose ends his reading of Stanislaw Lem's novel *Solaris* (1961) with stating that the narrative "serves as a confirmation that the nonhuman really exists, that beyond ourselves is something that is not ourselves, and as a reminder of the problematic nature of any interaction with the genuinely alien."[265] On a more theoretical note Istvan Csicsery-Ronay, Jr. has read the "negative apocalypse" of Darko Suvin's *novum* (briefly, a "new" object, like a time machine, that denotes a text as science fiction) as "lacks-made-solid" in the form of "mysterious objects and processes" which foreground the excess being discussed here.[266] The way that the moon in *Apollo 18* functions is as contact with the *never*-made-solid in the form of a moon which is always more than a moon (its rocks can always turn into killer spiders).

The film presents the fictional story of an Apollo 18 moon landing. The last actual landing was Apollo 17, which took place in 1972; although other missions were planned they were eventually canceled. The film "takes WikiLeaks as a distribution model"[267] by purporting to be edited from over 80 hours of secret footage uploaded to www.lunartruth.com, which is the official website of the movie. The footage shows that the Apollo 18 mission did in fact take place in 1974 and that it was kept hidden for a number of reasons, the main one being that all the crew members perished after being attacked by spider-like creatures on the lunar surface. The film is presented as an edit of the material uploaded, which mainly consists of images filmed by the astronauts themselves on the moon. Thus similar to the Russian pseudo-documentary about landing on the in moon in 1939, *First on the Moon* (2005), the film looks like a composite of different types of footage from different sources, all of which are purported to be real.[268] However, *Apollo 18* is different in that it almost entirely takes place on the moon and the moon itself becomes the strangest character in it.

[Cameras] For this type of "found footage" film one of the main concerns is to justify the footage that has been taken, as seen taking place in films such as *Cannibal Holocaust* (1980), *Man Bites Dog* (1992), *The Blair Witch Project* (1999) and so on.[269] This means that the camera as an object plays a significant role in the film, not only in the varying film stocks and aspect ratios used but also in the appearance of cameras themselves. However, rather than being a weak point in a film trying to locate itself in the found footage genre, the appearance of cameras in *Apollo 18* simply continues one of the major tropes found in lunar films from *Frau im Mond* onward, and that is the role of recording the moon while on the moon. Thus when an astronaut is shown framing a shot in the landing module or another sets up an unmanned camera fixed with a motion detector on the lunar surface there is nothing particularly out of place when taken in conjunction with purely fictitious images of cameras on the moon.

Yet rather than merely accounting for the authenticity of the footage, what all of this camera-work does is create a reason for the appearance of different starts and stutters of the actual material of the film on which the images are recorded. In other words, the medium of recording becomes an issue in the film, not just the fact that it was recorded in the first place. This can be seen throughout the film, but the first scene in which the spider-creatures attack an astronaut is a good example. The two astronauts on the surface of the moon, Commander Nate Walker (Lloyd Owen) and Captain Ben Anderson (Warren Christie), have found an empty Russian lunar lander and a dead cosmonaut. They worry for their own lives and try to take off from the moon surface but they find their radar is damaged. Walker makes an EVA to check out the problem. During this scene a number of effects are added to the image in order to simulate the different types of cameras used to record action in and around the lander, including interference, vertical linearity errors and over-saturation. These techniques create the kind of "haptic" looking that Laura Marks has outlined, meaning a kind of looking which tends to rest on the surface of its object rather than to plunge into depth, not to distinguish form so much as to discern texture. It is a labile, plastic sort of look, more inclined to move than to focus. The video works I propose to call haptic invite a look that moves on the surface plane of the screen for some time before the viewer realises what it is she is beholding. Haptic video resolves into figuration only gradually if at all, instead inviting the caressing look I have described.[270]

In order to keep the viewer's attention on the surface of the image a filmmaker can use "different processes, such as speeding up video footage in the film, enlarging the grain, and creating *mises-en-abîme* of video within film, to create a more or less optical or haptic sensation."[271] Such surface attention encourages a horizontal or planetary reading of film as *space* rather than looking for a vertical depth. In *Apollo 18* the tensions of the haptic spatial surface of the film mirrors the way that the entire surface of the moon becomes a site of tension in that every rock everywhere has the potential to kill.

[Rocks] Eventually astronaut Walker becomes infected by one of the spider-like lunar creatures. When he is bought back into the lunar module blood is seen to be seeping from his chest. Eventually an object is surgically removed by Anderson. What is removed is the object of horror in the film: a rock.

This rock seems to be an ordinary lunar rock, perhaps representing the lack of interesting objects found on the moon surface. It just sits on the table until Anderson taps it lightly with a hammer. Then it changes into an object of horror, exploding in blood. While at first this rock look like the "strange" bush in *Nude on the Moon* which was, to all intents and purposes, just a bush, in *Apollo 18* this rock is actually a spider-creature just waiting to pounce. It is from the ubiquitous nature of all rocks having the potential to be spiders that the horrific element of the film arises.

The reason that these images are haptic is because attention is brought to the texture of objects themselves, which cannot be trusted: dry rock has the potential to sprout spider legs and spurt blood. The reason these images are about space is that not all the rocks on the moon are rocks, but most of them are; therefore there is a tension between rocks and rocks which show how the image cannot be trusted, as it is unclear whether the lunar landscape is banal or deadly at any given moment. Thus rocks, which are ordinary, are also, and at the same time, extraordinary. This uncertainty then turns the whole surface of the planet into an uncanny site of terror. Thus there is a certain sense of a "flatness" of objects in the sense that everyday objects become horrific because "space" is becoming an issue, meaning, as Harman says speaking of the work of H.P. Lovecraft, that "visible objects display unbearable seismic torsion with their own qualities."[272] This horizontal tension is between the moon rocks and their qualities, which means between their "rockness" and their "stranger-than-rockness."

This kind of "spatial" threat is also seen near the end of López-Gallego's film when Anderson is finally able to escape the gravity of the lunar surface in the Soviet lander. Once he enters the moon's orbit and enters zero gravity the objects not bolted down in the module begin to float in the air. These objects are mainly lunar rocks. Some but not all of the rocks sprout legs and turn into lunar spiders, killing Anderson and causing his module to crash into the lunar orbiter, killing John Grey (Ryan Robbins), the astronaut inside. In this sense the threat in the film is spread out, equally everywhere, meaning it is located both in the micro-scale of individual rocks and in the macro-scale of the entire moon surface. While once again banal objects have become threatening, the question remains how this change from banal rock to deadly rock comes to be represented in moon films. This is taken up in the next chapter under the guise of seeing what remains hidden: the far side of the moon.

Chapter 15

Transformers 3 (2011), *Iron Sky* (2012)

[Seeing the Far Side] Lunar films have so far constructed a relationship to the dark side of the moon as that which cannot be seen. In a sense both Michael Bay's *Transformers 3: Dark of the Moon* (2011) and Timo Vuorensola's *Iron Sky* (2012) follow this pattern, locating both aliens and Nazis, respectively, in this dark corner. But the far side of the moon is actually something that is visible to us, and not just from orbiting satellites such as Luna 3 or from pictures taken by lunar landers: during a solar eclipse the far side blocks the sun while the near side in is shade, thus the light ring around the lunar edge which appears, or the annulus, is a bit of the dark side visible by the naked eye from Earth.

In *Seeing Dark Things* Roy Sorensen uses this fact to argue, in a seemingly paradoxical manner, that we do not see Near as much as we see Far: a star positioned in front of a sun is invisible because the brightness of the sun occludes it; thus the Far sun is easier for us to see than something Nearer than it.[273] Extending this argument, Sorensen puts forth that objects are not just passive things differentiated from their environment but rather that they need to be active in doing so: "Our conception of the physical mechanisms that support vision must be broadened to encompass the various kinds of visible dark objects. To include backlit objects, we must allow partial light blockage to count. Objects are *not* seen simply by virtue of a contrast with their environment. They must cause the contrast. That is the difference between Near and Far."[274] One way that Sorensen illustrates the manner in which objects are responsible for these contrasts rather than just the background is with an example well-known to lunar films, that of an astronaut in a rocket or on the moon seeing the coordinates of a sunrise reversed into an earthrise.[275] This illustrates Sorensen's argument because usually, in a sunrise for example, the movement of the earth is not noticed, just that of the sun; however, when an earthrise is seen from the moon the mobility of both objects is visible. In other words, both objects are seen to cause the contrast needed for their being noticed. Such activity is also necessary for things to be seen in the two films under discussion here: in *Transformers 3* this takes the form of simply "appearing from behind" while *Iron Sky* presents a more literal take on Sorensen's reading of seeing the far side of the moon during a solar eclipse when a hole blasted through the surface of the moon allows for the sun to be seen behind it.

[Been There] A short scene on the Transformers' home planet at the beginning of the film ends with one of their ships crash-landing on the moon. The ship is carrying a weapon which would help the good Autobot Transformers defeat the evil Decepticon Transformers once and for all. Recovering and using this weapon is the main plot of the film. The first shot of the lunar surface is a rapid pan to the right which whips by the earth hanging in the sky, so that it is hardly seen, in order to show the crashing space ship. This event is picked up by radar on Earth. A title shows that it is the year 1961 and scientists in an observatory hear the signals of the crash and contact the authorities. This date puts the event in the middle of a number of failed attempts in the late 1950s and early 1960s to launch a series of American lunar orbiters. However, as indicated above, images of the far side of the moon had already been taken by this time and were taken again thereafter. This means that in both *Transformers 3* and, as will be seen below, *Iron Sky*, somehow the alien ship/Nazi base have remained invisible, despite photographs of the dark side having been taken. One reason for this might be that these objects were not differentiated from their environment: they were like a bright light that is unseen when put in front of an even brighter light.

[In Back] In *Transformers 3* this moment of seeing what was hidden on the far side takes place on the surface of the moon. The signal of the crash did not provide information about what it was that hit the surface. This is shown to be the true impetus for President Kennedy launching the Apollo program. The Apollo 11 moon landing is presented, on the one hand, as having taken place just as history recorded it: actual footage of the take off and landing is shown and other elements are "faithfully" recreated.

However, eventually what lies "behind" the usual scenes shown from the moon is revealed. After Neil Armstrong lands, the NASA control center is shown. A switch is flipped and one of the controllers tells Armstrong: "Neil, you are dark on the rock, mission is a go." The famous shot of Armstrong reflected in Aldrin's helmet visor is shown. Then Armstrong turns around to look at what is behind him. It is at this point that the crashed object becomes visible: the alien spaceship is now reflected in Aldrin's visor. Once the ship is seen on the surface it can be fit into the language of moon films, the clearest sign of which is the ship appearing in a shot with the earth hanging above. Thus once the ship is seen with the astronauts' eyes it can be seen by the camera and fit into the genre conventions.

The mechanism for the object causing visibility in contrast to its environment in this sequence at first seems like a strange one, but it is *to appear from behind*. In Sorensen's example of the solar eclipse the "back" of the moon becomes visible as the "front" lies in shadow. He connects this to the way that the sun "in back" is visible while a star situated "in front" of it cannot be seen. Mixing film and reality it can be said that when the dark side of the moon was directly observed the alien ship was not visible to various pre-Apollo 11 NASA space craft, it was only when the ship appeared from behind the astronauts, or from behind the "actual" footage, that it begins to be seen. This "backward" way of viewing things fits into one of the main topics of this analysis of moon films, which is that the moon is only seen when it is seen indirectly. Here this indirectness is literalized in the "real" lunar events taking place just behind our backs, just out of sight.

[All Together] At the same time the horizontal aspect of indirectness is seen when, a bit later in the film, some of the Autobots go to the moon to retrieve the weapon. This scene depicts one of them walking up to the crashed ship through the debris of the Apollo missions. The Transformer makes its way between the crashed Autobot ship and the original lunar lander. In front of him are a number of lunar rovers, other instances of moon missions with a secondary purpose. This image has much in common with the multiple presentations of the moon in Méliès' film, at least on a theoretical level. What this image shows is one way the moon has been represented in moon films for over a century: in many ways at once. While in *Le Voyage* the different strategies took place over different shots here they are all shown together: Apollo moon lander, crashed alien space ship, Autobot visitor. In one sense this is a kind of "democracy" of different lunar experiences all shown together. What is important to remember, however, is that the moon is actually that which escapes all of these strategies. This point is taken up in the discussion of the next film.

[Summary] *Iron Sky* is also about something unseen located on the dark side of the moon. After the Second World War a number of Nazis have escaped undetected to the far side. This is similar to the plot of Robert Heinlein's novel *Rocketship Galileo* (1947), which was used as the basis for *Destination Moon* (minus the Nazis). In *Iron Sky*, the date is now 2018. The moon Nazis have continued in their beliefs and are now planning an invasion of Earth. Again, they are only detected on the moon when two astronauts are sent as a part of a feel-good mission to support the current president's re-election bid. Eventually war breaks out between the Nazis and the Americans.

There are two main examples of a horizontal tension in the film. The first is that on the feel-good mission to the moon one astronaut is shot and killed by a Nazi and the other is captured. Then, in the second, the Nazis are preparing to fire their ultimate weapon, the *Götterdämmerung*, at the earth but time is of the essence and they cannot see their target because the weapon is on the far side of the moon. Therefore, in order to "uncover" the earth and put it in the sites of their weapon the Nazis simply blow a hole through the landscape of the moon. It is through this hole that they are able to see the earth, although their plans for firing the weapon at it are eventually foiled. What both *Iron Sky* and *Transformers 3* indicate is that rather than an indirect approach to the "mere" an ontology is being presented in which all the narrative strategies take place on the flatness of the surface rather than in any kind of "in between" or deeper state of an object. This focuses on the operations or relations between objects rather than on objects themselves.

[Landing] The film opens with a pan following a space ship leaving Earth's orbit and entering that of the moon. The approach and landing of the ship follow familiar tropes of lunar films by always keeping the earth somewhere in frame. There is no mix of actual and fictional footage as in *Transformers 3*, thus there is no attempt to show a different history to that which is known by inserting new "unseen" footage into that which has been seen. In other words, *Transformers 3* shows what some people on Earth knew was going on all along—that the moon harbors signs of life from elsewhere. In *Iron Sky* history is also revised, as Nazis are shown having lived on the moon since World War II. However, no one on Earth knew this, they only find out in the present day of the film. Thus there is no historical footage to revise and the whole film can take place without an archive.

However, the firm location of the film in the present merely sets up its satirical nature. Upon landing the astronauts are required to unfurl campaign banners for the incumbent pseudo-Sarah Palin president, an act that they grudgingly perform. The plot of the film then becomes apparent: according to the public the single aim of the landing, the first since Apollo 17, is to put the first black man on the moon and thus boost votes from the African-American population in the upcoming election; however, the astronauts are also there to confirm the presence of Helium-3, a real-world (but rare on Earth) energy alternative to oil, meaning it could be used as a non-radioactive fuel for nuclear fission. Once on the surface of the moon the astronauts unwittingly discover the presence of the Nazis.

[First Contact] In Bay's film the presence of something alien on the moon is known before the first humans are sent there, thus the whole mission is constructed "with its back turned" to its real object. This position is illustrated in the famous scene of Armstrong seen in the reflection of Aldrin's helmet visor: after this moment is reenacted Aldrin turns around and the alien ship takes Armstrong's place. In *Iron Sky* a similar moment is set up. Two astronauts have landed on the moon: James Washington (Christopher Kirby) is merely a propaganda tool, "a pretty face" he calls himself; Sanders (Ben Siemer) is a scientist secretly looking for Helium-3. As Sanders explores the moon in search of the precious resource he makes his way to the top of a ridge. It is here that the reflection-in-the-visor scene takes place. However, the key difference in this scene is that although Sanders stops, obviously arrested by something that he sees, this object cannot be made out from the visor reflection. In addition, the next shot, which, according to film logic of the classical narrative variety, should be matched to the POV of Sanders and show what he is seeing, is not. Instead it shows Washington seeing Sanders but not seeing what Sanders is seeing. It is only then that what Sanders sees is shown, although this is done from an angle which does not match the line of sight of Washington, instead it is from a high over-the-shoulder shot which reveals the Nazi Helium-3 plant. Yet there is one more "surprise" in this sequence. When Sanders turns back to Washington while explaining what he sees, a moon Nazi sneaks up over his shoulder and shoots him.

While in *Transformers 3* viewing the actual moon took place "from behind" the moon footage as we know it, in *Iron Sky* it takes place in a multitude of manners: in front of, far away from, below and behind. This multitude of viewpoints sometimes does not follow the expectations of standard Hollywood editing, and thus begins to lend itself to what Shaviro calls a loss of "the active mastery of the gaze,"[276] meaning that the viewer begins to lose their sense of localization. At the same time, the gathering of these different viewpoints together can be understood in relation to the edge of the far side of the moon becoming visible during a solar eclipse. Above it was argued that when the sun appears behind the moon (relative to Earth) in a solar eclipse the near side of the moon appears in shadow. However, there is a small rim around the edge of the moon which becomes visible by being back-lit. This argument was used to show that we see "behind" more clearly than we see "in front." In *Transformers 3* the alien ship is on the dark side of the moon. Action on the dark side takes place "behind" the near side in the sense that the cameras that recorded the moon landing as we know it were all turned away from the ship. Thus the real action of the moon took place "behind" what we know of it. However, according to Sorenson's theory, there is a chance that this background information could become seen in the foreground. If the history that Bay's film is proposing were true this would become obvious. Think of the detailed analysis offered by the proponents of moon landing hoax theories such as Collier. They would easily be able to discover that only "half" the moon had been shown, meaning that the cameras only showed a range of 180º. In this way the alien ship would be seen in that something would have been obviously hidden by the actual moon footage.

When Sanders approaches the ridge something catches his attention and this something is reflected in his visor. However, it is rather hard to see exactly what it is. In the next cut Washington sees Sanders but Washington does not see what is behind Sanders. In the solar eclipse configuration this would place Washington is the position of Earth, Sanders in the position of the moon and the Nazi quarry in the place of the sun. This configuration is supported by the fact that the sun appears behind Sanders in the upper-right-hand corner of the screen. Although the three elements are not exactly in line in the form of a syzygy, the end of the film shows a similar configuration with a shot of the moon in front of the sun, as seen from the point of view of the earth. Examining this last scene will help develop an understanding of the function of the moon throughout the film.

[Hole in the Moon] As stated above, near the end of the film the Nazis head their ultimate weapon, the *Götterdämmerung*, toward the earth. However, there is not enough time to bring the huge ship around the far side of the moon to get a clear line of sight so it blows a hole through the edge of the moon instead. This offers an image in line with the dissolves seen in *Destination Moon*, which is that of seeing one object in another. In the chapter on *Destination Moon* the argument was made that seeing an object "through" another made a case for the presence of theatricality within the film. Theatricality, following the thought of Samuel Weber, was seen as presencing action over place. This was then connected to a discussion of Bergson's *durée* and his critique of cinema. However, this discussion was undertaken through the technique of the dissolve, which is absent here. Instead a different operation is in play: the moon *makes way* for the earth. This making-way is a *granting* of space where it is not deserved, such as a car slowing down for another which is cutting in line. Thus *this action is one of hesitation*. In the chapter on *Paper Moon* Meillassoux was cited as saying that "'hesitant' code is not the pure and simple absence of a code, but a hesitation between two options that are now equally likely." In *Iron Sky* hesitation allows the unseen (Earth) to come forth, although it takes place completely within the realm of fantasy, or camp, which has its own horizontal access to truth.

[Eclipse] The last scene of the film shows the Earth/Moon/Sun in alignment of a solar eclipse, but with a difference. First the sun is seen appearing behind the moon, although because of the hole in its side more of the sun is seen than usual. The issue this shot raises for the idea of seeing "from behind" is that when the background shines through the foreground it is no longer merely the foreground which needs to "cause" its own visibility to take place but the background becomes "active" too. This can be seen in further shots of the sun behind the moon in which it over-reaches its position of "behind" and overtakes the edge of the moon completely. This is the last shot of the film, which also includes nuclear detonations going off across the surface of the earth. What these images show is a sun that is no longer contained by the moon. Instead the moon has let the background loose. It has done this through the process of "making way" for another object. What the moon does is let what is beyond be seen. The strategies for doing so have been various, but in this scene the moon acts more like a window than a door.

Conclusion

Moon (2009)

[Moon-Earth Relations] The films collated under the rubric of "moon films" have shown that putting the object of the moon on screen demands multiple techniques of representation to be used together. This gathering of techniques creates a horizontal gap or tension between these representations. This gap is what indirectly generates lunar truth. This was seen in the cubism of *Le Voyage*, in the mix of fact and fantasy in both camp films and those made just before the lunar landing, in the difficulty in reading actual moon footage and in the way that films made after the lunar landing interrogated images of the moon rather than the moon itself. What all these films have in common is that putting the moon on film makes what is strange even stranger.

Duncan Jones' *Moon* (2009) both fits into this series of films and provides a fitting end to the text in that strangeness comes about in the manner in which Earth and Moon are screened as ontological equals, a strategy which is also reflected in the way that the main protagonist struggles with the discovery that he has an equal himself; in other words, he finds out that he is "merely" a clone.

Sam Bell (Sam Rockwell) is the sole employee on a moon base which has been set up to mine lunar rock of Helium-3, just as in *Iron Sky*. Bell is at the end of his three-year contract and about to return to Earth. The first sign that something is wrong is when he begins to hallucinate and see visions of his daughter. The second time this happens is in the midst of debris thrown up by one of the automated Helium-3 harvesters; Bell loses control of his rover and crashes.

The Bell that is next shown waking up in an infirmary at the moon base is quickly seen to be a clone, as is thus the first Bell who is lying unconscious in the rover. A stock of Bells is kept by the mining company to run the moon station, although they are unaware of this and are implanted with false memories. However, once the second Bell rescues the first their status as clones is revealed to them and the main issue of interest here is raised, that of different objects being equal to each other. This equality is initially seen in the manner in which the two Bells overcome their initial hostility toward each other and begin working together. Initially the first Bell wants to be friends with the second and asks to shake hands. This initial invitation is declined, although eventually, as the first Bell's heath declines, the second warms up to him, and the new Bell puts his hand on the old Bell's forehead.

This scene is not just about emotions, however, but also about two objects which are the same (two Sam Bells) and which are taking place together on screen. This is not an example of co-presencing but rather of Harman's horizontal tension, in which a sensual object is in tension with its sensual qualities. This was also called "space." The sensual object in this case is Bell, although in fact it could be any Bell, since neither of them is the first Bell. However, this sensual object is put in conflict with its own qualities by being repeated, or by being shown with itself on screen. Tension comes forth in the way that the two Bells learn how similar they are, meaning what little separates them. While this kind of doubling is no stranger to fiction, what becomes interesting in *Moon* is that it is not limited to the clones. For example, there are a number of cutaway shots of the moon which are used to show the passage of time. Most of them show computer-generated graphics of the moon, Earth and Sun in relation to each other. However, twice a different kind of image is shown, that of the moon-as-picture, which is indicated by the tell-tale "cross-hairs" of a camera.

Such images are "horizontal" because the crosshairs mark it as a representation of the moon in the midst of presentations of it—

the latter being unmarked as images within the film; at the same time this cross-hair moon is being positioned as a presentation in the manner in which it is used as a cutaway rather than as a picture a character is looking at in the deigesis, as was seen with the lunar map in *The Cosmic Voyage*. What this does in *Moon* is put the cutaway in tension with itself, since it is a representation in the position of a presentation. In other words, both the sensual moon (presentation) and its qualities (as a picture) are shown to be equal. This is what Manuel DeLanda has called a "*flat ontology*," which he describes as an ontology "made exclusively of unique, singular individuals, differing in spatio-temporal scale but not in ontological status."[277] The context for his discussion is equating an individual with a species, the latter being "just another individual entity, one which operates at larger spatio-temporal scales."[278] The operation which takes place when an individual is not confined to the individual scale is a kind of "planetary" awareness. Eugene Thacker has developed the manner in which this kind of planetary awareness works, although he has done it through a reading of black metal music.

[Black Metal] Black Metal music, at least according to the definition of the heavy metal sub-genre provided by Thacker in *In the Dust of This Planet,* suggests three ways in which the objects exceed each other in the language used above. All three are derived from the different meaning of "black" in black metal.

First, *black* can mean Satanism, which "is governed by a structure of opposition and inversion";[279] this can be seen in the way that Satanic rituals are constructed as the opposite of canonical Christian ones. Second, *black* can mean Paganism, which is governed by a structure of "exclusion and alterity,"[280] meaning a kind of polytheism. Third, and most important for this study, *black* can mean Cosmic Pessimism, which consists of a "dark metaphysics of negation, nothingness, and the nonhuman."[281] In distinction to the first two kinds of black, Cosmic Pessimism can be seen as an attempt to think of the world before, beyond and in excess of humanity, where "There is only the anonymous, impersonal 'in itself' of the world, indifferent to us as human beings, despite all we do to change, to shape, to improve, and even to save the world... Its limit-thought is the idea of absolute nothingness, unconsciously represented in the many popular media images of nuclear war, natural disasters, global pandemics, and the cataclysmic effects of climate change."[282] Black Pessimism terms an object "which still exists, but simply without relation to anything else";[283] thus it is a prime contender for "space" as it is being used here.

Although he does not make an explicit connection between the two at this point in his text, Thacker has another term for this pessimistic type of Black Metal, and that is *planet*: "the world-without-us is simply the *Planet*.... What is important in the concept of the Planet is that it remains a negative concept, simply that which remains 'after' the human. The Planet can thus be described as impersonal and anonymous."[284] Thacker's negative concept of Planet is one way of understanding the manner in which one object exceeds another: a planet is always beyond humanity, never caring about humanity, larger than our grasp, and so on. Planets, as Timothy Morton says, "have Gaussian geometry and measurable spacetime distortion because they are so massive"; in other words, "They are really old and really huge compared with humans."[285] Planetary features are too wide-spread, too slow or too fast to be noticed by direct observation, yet they are not opaque: we now have the technological means to begin seeing things on a planetary scale, so that no matter where we are global warming wreaks deadly havoc on the coasts of Japan and Indonesia or the storage of radioactive waste raises questions of who gets stuck with storing it and how it is connected to everyone everywhere. Thus the "historical moment" in which such inhuman scales are becoming visible to humanity is upon us;[286] the question is what we do with it.[287] The planetary becomes visible, as Harman describes, in the "splitting a thing off as a dark, brooding unit in distinction from its palpable qualities";[288] in other words, in horizontal tension. This splitting off was seen in its most literal sense in the "Breakaway" episode of *Space: 1999*. In Duncan Jones' *Moon* it takes on a different aspect: the earth is split off from its main function in moon films, a placeholder for the idea of home.

[The Earth is Not Your Home] This splitting off is seen in what looks like one of the most frequent lunar images that have appeared in this study, that of the earth seen from the moon surface, although in actuality no image like it has been seen before.

In this sequence the first Bell is getting ill. He is still trying to believe in the actuality of his having a wife and child on Earth, although the second Bell shares the same memories of them. Communication with Earth is possible but only through recorded video because supposedly a communication satellite is down. Eventually the Bells discover that the live signal is being jammed and the first Bell takes a lunar rover out beyond the reach of the jammers; he is able to make contact with his family. He finds out that his wife is dead and that his daughter is now a teenager. Before making contact with what is presumably the original Bell the first Bell cuts the connection. Bell cries and is frustrated, knowing that he is forever cut off from what he thought was his family. It is then that the image of the earth in the moon sky is shown.

Because their moon base is located on the far side of the moon the Bells have never had a reason nor the ability to travel to the near side. Thus this is the first and only time that the earth is shown from the moon. However, rather than the earth being a normalizing force as it was in *2001*, for example, here it becomes strange. The earth is "not home." In this sense the moon and the earth are here equal in ontological status: both are seen as objects floating in space. Perhaps this is the most that can be asked of moon films. Yet it is not that dreaming about the moon, envisioning landing on it, and then effecting a landing has now somehow equalized the two objects by bringing the moon into the earth's sphere of scientific understanding; instead the moon is shown to have a much stronger effect by making the strangeness of the earth an issue. In other words, the moon encourages presentational strategies to be in tension with each other. Due to the fact that seeing the earth "floating in space" arises from strategies of imagining the lunar, it can be said that the films under discussion here have actually turned the earth into a piece of the moon.

Endnotes

1 Scott Montgomery, *The Moon and the Western Imagination* (Tucson: University of Arizona Press, 1999), 117.

2 Much information about the film was gathered by the BFI as a part of their "75 Most Wanted Films" project, however, now the website is only available in archived form, John Oliver, "The First Men in the Moon," British Film Institute (2011), Internet: http://web.archive. org/web/20110910 121426/http://www.BFI.org.UK/nationalarchive/news/most wanted/first-men-in-the-moon.html.

3 These "Selenites" actually reflect aspects of Wells' original description of them, which includes: "blank black figure"; "somewhat hunchbacked, with a high forehead and long features"; and "It seemed as though it wasn't a face; as though it must be a mask, a horror, a deformity that would presently be disavowed or explained. There was no nose, and the thing had bulging eyes at the side—in the silhouette I had supposed they were ears.... I have tried to draw one of these heads but I cannot," *The Strand Magazine* 21 (1901), 168.

4 Qtd. in Oliver, "The First Men."

5 Graham Harman, *Weird Realism: Lovecraft and Philosophy* (Hants: Zero Books, 2012), 51.

6 The curvature could perhaps even suggest the use of the "gravity assist" method for escaping Earth's orbit, a concept not developed until 1918 (16 years after Méliès' film) by Yuri Kondratyuk. See Richard Dowling et al, "The Origin of Gravity-Propelled Interplanetary Space Travel," in *History of Rocketry and Astronautics*, J.D. Huntly, ed. (San Diego: American Astronautical Society, 1997): 63-102. In addition, when the astronomers leave the moon at the end of *Le Voyage*, their capsule drops off a steep cliff and then goes

"straight down," landing in one of Earth's oceans. Perhaps this could also be taken as a metaphor for a way in which the capsule could escape the gravitational pull of a large body using a "free-fall" method rather than rocket propulsion. This is a contrary reading to what Dona Jalufka and Christian Koeberl conclude in perhaps a too literal reading in "Moonstruck: How Realistic is the Moon Depicted in Classic Science Fiction Films?" when they state that "Gravitation, well known since the late 1600s, is wrongly depicted (the fall of the capsule from the moon to the earth)," *Earth, Moon and Planets* 85-6 (2001), 182.

7 Elizabeth Ezra argues for the importance of this overlapping editing in Méliès' *A la conquête du Pôle/Conquest of the Pole* (1912), *George Méliès* (Manchester: Manchester University Press, 2000), 33. In 1908, Segundo de Chomón made *Excursion en la Luna*, an imitation of *Le Voyage*. In de Chomón's version, the capsule is shown flying into the mouth of the Man in the Moon. It is swallowed and then the Man in the Moon spits fire out of his mouth. The capsule is then shown already having landed on the moon in the next shot.

8 Marjorie Hope Nicolson, *Voyages to the Moon* (New York: The Macmillan Company, 1960), 45.

9 In "Shooting the Moon from Outer Space: Reframing Modern Vision," Tom Gunning develops a reading of what he calls "rocket vision" in *Le Voyage* which he distinguishes from the "modern vision" of the beginning of the 20th century, in *Fantastic Voyages of the Cinematic Imagination: Georges Méliès's Trip to the Moon*. Edited by Mathew Solomon (Albany: State University of New York Press, 2011). Gunning's thought is taken up numerous times in this chapter.

10 In *War and Cinema: The Logistics of Perception* Paul Virilio argues that it is actually a penchant for destruction in the

cinema of Méliès which is the reason for some action being shown twice, such as the moon landing (London; New York: Verso, 1999), 13-4.

11 Tom Gunning uses the rocket POV shot to argue that *Le Voyage* illustrates "rocket vision": "More than simply indicating a view, the shot makes palpable a trajectory. In effect, this is a peculiarly technological and modern viewpoint, the viewpoint of the speeding rocket. ... Technologically mediated vision fascinated early cinema, portraying a peculiarly modern perception. The conjunction of vision and devices wittily doubled the cinema's own medium of viewing and foregrounded the act of display by framing it," "Shooting the Moon from Outer Space," 106. I am not so interested in this "type" of vision but rather in the multiplicity of many types of vision seen in the film.

12 Graham Harman, *Circus Philosophicus* (Hants: Zero Books, 2010), 63.

13 Harman, *Wierd Realism*, 4.

14 Ibid., 5.

15 Siegfried Kracauer, *Theory of Film: The Redemption of Physical Reality* (New York: Oxford University Press, 1966), 30-7. Or, perhaps more instructively, this is the difference between what Tom Gunning calls Lumièr's realistic illusion and Méliès' magical illusion, "The Cinema of Attraction: Early Film, Its Spectator, and the Avant-Garde," *Wide Angle* 8:3-4 (Fall 1986), 64.

16 André Gaudreault, "Theatricality, Narrativity, and 'Trickality': Reevaluating the Cinema of Georges Méliès," *Journal of Popular Film and Television* 15:3 (Fall 1987), 113.

17 Martin Heidegger, "Building Dwelling Thinking," in *Basic Writings*, ed. David Farrell Krell (New York: HarperCollins, 1993), 351.

18 Thus I do not read the images of the moon in *Le Voyage* as "going beyond" Heidegger as Gunning claims in "Shooting

the Moon from Outer Space," 107, but rather as coming out of his thought and foregrounding some of its less-developed elements.

19 Heidegger, "Building Dwelling Thinking," 353.

20 Heidegger says, "mortals nurse and nurture the things that grow, and specially construct things that do not grow. Cultivating and construction are building in the narrower sense. Dwelling, in as much as it keeps the fourfold in things, is, as this keeping, a building," Ibid. However, as Derrida has shown, for Heidegger such a human dwelling in the world has a linguistic base which basically means they can take it apart and put it together in ways that creatures without speech cannot, Jacques Derrida, *Aporias*, trans. Thomas Dutoit (Stanford: Stanford University Press, 1993), 36.

21 In *Hopkins and Heidegger* I claim that *das Geviert* was an important interpretive strategy because the four terms were allowed to negate each other (London; New York: Continuum, 2009), 80-1; here I argue that their mere presence together can be important.

22 Ibid.

23 Harman, *Wierd Realism*, 16.

24 Tom Gunning, "The Cinema of Attractions," 64. Although *Le Voyage* is Gunning's central reference for his cinema, in a later piece he gives more space to an analysis of the film's storyline, while still stressing its exhibitionist style, "Lunar Illuminations," in *Film Analysis: A Norton Reader*, ed. Jeffrey Geiger and R. L. Rutsky (New York: Norton, 2003), esp. 71-6

25 Gunning, "The Cinema of Attractions," 66.

26 Ibid.

27 Ibid.

28 For Harman, this point is used to argue that because some objects are unaffected by certain situations (such as an oil tanker not shifting course when a passenger on it bursts into

tears) objects therefore exist outside human relations (or thought), *Circus Philosophicus*, 70-1.

29 Harman, "The Well-Wrought Broken Hammer," *New Literary History* 43 (2012), 192.

30 Gunning could be re-inserted here, stressing that he uses the plural for "attraction" in his concept, and thus we could read an unthought element of horizontal presencing in his essay, which is later developed in his "Shooting the Moon in Outer Space," although also in a relatively tangential fashion.

31 Mathew Solomon, "Introduction," *Fantastic Voyages of the Cinematic Imagination: Georges Méliès's Trip to the Moon*, ed. Mathew Solomon (Albany: State University of New York Press, 2011), 6. This horizontal strategy was also seen in the presencing of craters and a face together in the moon.

32 Max Fleischer's animated *Dancing on the Moon* (1935) features a similar appearance of Man in the Moon's face upon approach, but the rocket simply passes by to the far side of the moon for its landing and the face disappears.

33 Gunning, "Lunar Illuminations," 77.

34 Gaudreault argues, against Georges Sadoul, that such multiplicity is a key aspect of Méliès' work as a whole, "Theatricality, Narrativity, and 'Trickality,'" 116.

35 Gunning, "Shooting the Moon in Outer Space," 108.

36 Harman, "The Well-Wrought Broken Hammer," 195.

37 Montgomery, *The Moon and the Western Imagination*, 39.

38 Gunning, "Lunar Illuminatinos," 72.

39 Gaudreault, "Theatricality, Narrativity and 'Trickality,'" 113.

40 Murray Pomerance, "'Distance Does Not Exist': Méliès, le Cinéma, and the Moon," in *Fantastic Voyages of the Cinematic Imagination: Georges Méliès's Trip to the Moon*, ed. Mathew Solomon (Albany: State University of New York Press, 2011), 95.

41 Stan Brakhage takes the opposite approach, arguing that the "underground" aspect of Méliès indicates his ability to make the hidden visible: "Thus George became the first man to recognize motion pictures as medium of both super-nature and under-world—an instrument for unveiling the natural through reflection... and also the gateway for an alien world underneath the surface of our natural visual ability—an underworld that erupts into 'ours' through every machine which makes visible to us what we cannot naturally sense," *The Brakhage Lectures: Georges Méliès, David Wark Griffith, Carl Theodore Dreyer, Sergei Eisenstein* (Chicago: The GoodLion, 1972), 14.

42 Harman, "The Well-Wrought Broken Hammer," 186.

43 Gunning, "Shooting the Moon in Outer Space," 108.

44 Bernd Brunner, *Moon: A Brief History* (New Haven; London: Yale University Press, 2010), 212.

45 Another indication of the personal nature of the Professor's involvement in representations of the moon is that in addition to the scientific papers hung about, the Professor has himself made a number of drawings directly onto the walls of his apartment, thus expressing his "obsessive" attitude toward the moon. The fact that the Professor's current research on the moon appears on the walls of his apartment rather than in scientific publications further delineates his position as outcast from the scientific community.

46 Marie Lathers, *Space Oddities: Women and Outer Space in Popular Film and Culture: 1960-2000* (London; New York: Continuum, 2010), 3.

47 Tom Gunning, *The Films of Fritz Lang: Allegories of Vision and Modernity* (London: British Film Institute, 2008), 173.

48 For a summary of the role of scientific knowledge in *Frau im Mond* see David Kirby, *Lab Coats in Hollywood: Science, Scientists, and Cinema* (Cambridge: MIT Press, 2010), 97-8.

Knowledge about a lack of atmosphere on the moon was available long before Lang, see Brunner, *Moon*, 18-9.

49 Quentin Meillassoux, *After Finitude: An Essay on the Necessity of Contingency*, trans. Ray Brassier (London; New York: Continuum, 2006), 9.

50 Ibid., 13.

51 Ibid., 22.

52 Ibid.

53 Ibid., 24-6.

54 Laurence Rickels, *Nazi Psychoanalysis: Volume III, Psy-Fi* (Minneapolis: University of Minnesota Press, 2002), 139.

55 Gunning, *The Films of Fritz Lang*, 173. However, in *Film as Art* Rudolf Arnheim uses an example from *Frau im Mond* to illustrate characterization: "Thus an external event, some little piece of action, is invented which reflects the mental state of the actor. When, in Woman in the Moon, Willy Fritsch with his paper shears cuts the heads off the flowers standing in a vase on his desk while he is telephoning, his gesture shows much more clearly than his facial expression how agitated he is. Moreover it is real film stuff (even though elementary) because it is action, visible action" (Berkeley: University of California Press, 1957), 140.

56 Qtd. in Gunning, *The Films of Fritz Lang*, 174.

57 Ibid.

58 Jacques Rivette, "The Hand," in Jim Hiller, ed., *Cahiers du Cinéma: The 1950s: Neo-realism, Hollywood, New Wave* (Cambridge: Harvard University Press, 1985), 140.

59 Ibid., 141.

60 Ibid.

61 Bellour, "On Fritz Lang," *SubStance* 3:9 (1974), 31.

62 Raymond Bellour, "On Fritz Lang," 28. Perhaps the quintessential example of this in Lang's films is in *M* (1931) when a mother's screams for her missing child are shown to reverberate through an empty stairwell and cut with pictures of

the lunch set out for the daughter who will not arrive, see Kracauer, *Theory of Film,* 122.

63 Bellour, "On Fritz Lang," 33. These gaps appear in a number of places. For example, a gap between subject and object is visualized when, as Bellour argues, the crowd of spectators observing the take-off of the rocket mutates into the group of scientists on the rocket observing the moon and sun out of their window; this foregrounds the manner in which both groups are separated from their object by being locked into a point of view, Raymond Bellour, *Le corps du cinéma: Hypnoses, émotions, animalités* (Paris: P.O.L., 2009), 72.

64 Friedrich Kittler locates a different gap in this scene in his *Optical Media,* that between the silent-era Professor and the sound-era scientists with him on the mission: "Funnily enough, one of the last German silent films, which had actually been made in the era of sound film, illustrated the difference between the two media within the plot as the difference between two generations. Using expressionistic silent film gestures, Fritz Lang's 1929 film *Frau im Mond* (*Woman in the Moon*) depicted an old, poverty-stricken professor who dreams only theoretically of moon rockets. In contrast, the younger engineers, who turned this theory into blitzkrieg technology at practically the same time as the real Wernher von Braun, are depicted with the economical gestures of sound film, the new objectivity, and the Wehrmacht," trans. Anthony Enns (Cambridge; Mladen: Polity Press, 2012), 202.

65 Gean Moreno, "Editorial: 'Accelerationist Aesthetics,'" *e-flux* 46 (Summer 2013), Internet: http://www.e-flux.com/journa /editorial%E2%80%94%E2%80%9Caccelerationist-aesth etics%E2%80%9D/. This editorial comes from an issue Moreno edited on accelerationism.

66 John Mullarkey, *Philosophy and the Moving Image: Refractions of Reality* (London: Palgrave Macmillan, 2010), 163.

67 Ibid., 173.

68 Benjamin Noys, The *Persistence of the Negative: A Critique of Contemporary Continental Theory* (Edinburgh: Edinburgh University Press, 2010), 5. Cf. Alex Williams and Nick Srnicek, "#Accelerate Manifesto for an Accelerationist Politics," *Critical Legal Thinking* (14 May, 2013), Internet: http://criticallegalthinking.com/2013/05/14/accelerate-manifesto-for-an-accelerationist-politics/.

69 Steven Shaviro, *Post Cinematic Affect* (Hants: Zero Books, 2010), 136-8.

70 Benedict Singleton, "Maximum Jailbreak," *e-flux* 46 (Summer 2013), Internet: http://www.e-flux.com/journal/maximum-jailbreak/.

71 Although Paul Virilio would read it as another example of the "vision machine."

72 In a similar manner David Mindell focuses his work in *Digital Apollo* on the relationship between human and computer in the Apollo program: "Would the exigencies of rockets, supersonic flight, and split-second decisions, not to mention onboard computers, threaten the classical heroic qualities? What tasks were susceptible to human skill, and what was too fast, complex, or uncertain for a human to intervene? How were Apollo designers to engineer a system that had a place for a heroic operator? As Apollo's machines were designed, built, and operated they called the very nature of 'heroism' into question. What did it mean to be in control?" (Cambridge: MIT Press, 2008), 13.

73 In an interview from 1965 Lang describes the strangeness engendered, many years after making *Frau im Mond*, by seeing actual photographs of the dark side of the moon: "In 1959 we saw the dark side of the moon. A Soviet photo showed the entire world something which no one had ever seen. It was the most sensational event of the year, remember? Whoever doubted photography would be part

of progress couldn't any longer. The camera on a lunar rocket recorded, transmitted, confirmed. But what had really happened? What was brought to us in those pictures of the dark side of the moon? The question is still unanswered," *Fritz Lang: Interviews*, ed. Barry Grant (Jackson: University of Mississippi Press, 2003), 60. These images, taken by the Soviet Luna 3 orbiter, are taken up below.

74 This is an extreme version of what Bellour identifies as the varying "distance at which the camera is held" which defines an unstable position of the author in Lang's films, "On Fritz Lang," 34.

75 My reading does not engage in psychoanalytic takes on the film. *In Lost in Space: Probing Feminist Science Fiction and Beyond* Marleen Barr connects the water used to cool the ship in the launch sequence of the film as a metaphor for birthing and hence mothering (Chapel Hill: University of North Carolina Press, 1993), 115-6; in a similar manner Tom Gunning sees the idea of "separation" in the film as that between the mother (Earth) and the child (those on the rocket), *The Films of Fritz Lang*, 174-5.

76 Boris Groys traces the history of the space supposed to be occupied by the palace, meaning the construction, demolition and re-construction of the Cathedral of Christ the Savior in *Art Power* (Cambridge: MIT Press, 2013), 158-63.

77 This argument is also supported by the fact that the first shot after the opening credits of the animated remake of *The Cosmic Voyage, Polet na Lunu/The Flight to the Moon* (1953), a rather New York-looking skyline is shown with a moon blazing in the corner, a feature argued to be missing from the earlier film. It would seem that such an immediate representation of the moon would negate any resistance to representation in the animated version; however, this would be a

rash judgment. For while the animated remake offers numerous scientific illustrations of the moon in its opening scenes, when a scientist is seen looking intently through a telescope at an observatory no corresponding image of the moon is matched to his gaze, just as in *The Cosmic Voyage*.

78 In a sense this is reminiscent of James Nasmyth's faked lunar landscapes which are generally presented piecemeal and in close-up in his 1874 *The Moon: Considered as a Planet, a World, and a Satellite*. See Frances Robertson, "Science and Fiction: James Nasmyth's Photographic Images of the Moon," *Victorian Studies* 48:4 (Summer 2006): 595-623.

79 Jane Grant, "Soft Moon: Exploring Matter and Mutability in Narratives and Histories of the Earth-Moon System," *Leonardo* 46:5 (2013), 435.

80 Graham Harman, *Quentin Meillassoux: Philosophy in the Making* (Edinburgh: Edinburgh University Press, 2011), 147.

81 Ibid., 149.

82 Ibid., 148. In an interview from 2011 Harman puts it thus: "Objects are paradoxes, because they are more than their subcomponents but less than their effects on other things. Objects live on the mezzanine level of the world. Or rather, there are countless mezzanine levels in the world, because a proton is an object no less than a horse is," *Ask/Tell* (October 23, 2011), Internet: http://eeevee2.blogspot.com/2011/10/interview-with-graham-harman.html.

83 Harman, *Quentin Meillassoux*, 148.

84 Meillassoux, *After Finitude*, 19.

85 See Graham Harman, "Meillassoux's Virtual Future," *Continent* 1:2 (2011), 82-3.

86 Meillassoux, *After Finitude*, 20.

87 Harman also uses the moon in another context, to illustrate a point from Meillassoux's *The Divine Inexistence*. This is taken up below.

88 Brunner, *Moon*, 60.

89 James Attlee, *Nocturne: A Journey in Search of Moonlight* (Chicago: University of Chicago Press, 2011), 308.

90 Qtd. in ibid., 77-8.

91 Ibid., 79.

92 Walter Benjamin, "One-Way Street," in *Selected Writings: 1913-1926*, trans. Edmund Jephcott, eds. Marcus Bullock and Michael Jennings (Cambridge: Harvard University Press, 1996), 476.

93 Miriam Bratu Hansen, "Benjamin and Cinema: Not a One-Way Street," *Critical Inquiry* 25 (Winter 1999), 317.

94 Ibid., 320.

95 This prompts Hank Davis to claim that "Some of the scenes, impressive as they may be, have become as familiar as the faces of Republic's team of actors," Classic *Cliffhangers: Volume 2, 1941-1955* (Baltimore: Midnight Marquee Press, 2008), 208.

96 Susan Sontag, "Notes on 'Camp,'" in *Against Interpretation and other Essays* (New York: Picador, 1970), 288.

97 Matthew Tinkcom, *Working Like a Homosexual: Camp, Captial, Cinema* (Durham: Duke University Press, 2002), 97.

98 Greg Taylor, *Artists in the Audience: Cults, Camp and American Film Criticism* (Princeton: Princeton University Press, 1999), 52.

99 Andrew Ross, "Uses of Camp," in *Camp Grounds: Style and Homosexuality*, ed. David Bergman (Amherst: University of Massachusetts Press, 1993), 58.

100 Jalufka and Koeberl, "Moonstruck," 186.

101 Philip Core, *Camp: The Lie that Tells the Truth* (Medford: Plexus, 1996).

102 Meillassoux calls this position "pre-critical" because ever since Kant it has been impossible to ignore the claim of transcendental idealism which states that humans cannot escape thought to see what lies beyond it. Meillassoux then coins the term correlationism for this position because

arguments after Kant state that everything known is correlated to humanity's thoughts or perceptions of the world, *After Finitude*, 5.

103 See M. Keith Booker, "Science Fiction and the Cold War," in *A Companion to Science Fiction*, ed. David Seed (Mladen: Blackwell, 2005).

104 Jan Alan Henderson, "Brothers from Another Planet: The Lydeckers," *American Cinematographer* 72:12 (1991), 163.

105 Ben Woodard, *Slime Dynamics* (Hants: Zero Books, 2012), 66.

106 Ibid., 12.

107 Ibid., 9.

108 Graham Harman, "On Vicarious Causation," *Collapse* 2 (2007), 190. In this sense the moon could take the form of one of Timothy Morton's hyperobjects, some of which are "molten." These objects are so large that they put assumptions regarding the linearity of space and time into question, "Sublime Objects," *Speculations* 2 (2011): 207-227. In a post from December 21, 2010, on Morton's blog *Ecology Without Nature* he mentions seeing a "blood moon" effect caused by a lunar eclipse thus: "I thought it fit to see a gigantic object, the planet we standing on, blocking the sun's light from the moon. Dance of the hyperobjects," Internet: http://ecologywithoutnature.blogstpot.com/2010/12/blood-moon-html?m=1.

109 Attlee, *Nocturnes*, 5.

110 Siegfried Kracauer says of *Frau im Mond*: "The lunar landscape smelled distinctly of Ufa's Neubabelsberg studios," *From Caligari to Hitler: A Psychological History of the German Film* (New York: Princeton University Press, 1947), 151.

111 Jane Bennett, *Vibrant Matter: A Political Ecology of Things* (Durham; London: Duke University Press, 2010), 104.

112 In distinction to this scene in the 1959 remake of *Cat-Women* by Richard Cunha, *Missile to the Moon*, in which the sighting

of the moon causes all of the space travellers to huddle around the view-screen to see it.

113 Tinkcom, *Working Like a Homosexual*, 28.

114 Brassier, Iain Hamilton Grant, Graham Harman and Quentin Meillassoux, "Speculative Realism," *Collapse* 3 (2007), 373.

115 Harman, *Circus Philosophicus*, 72.

116 Lathers, *Space Oddities*, 163.

117 Montgomery, *The Moon and the Western Imagination*, 50-2.

118 Mary Ann Doane, *Femmes Fatales: Feminism, Film Theory, Psychoanalysis* (New York; London: Routledge, 1991), 3.

119 Ibid., 116.

120 Quentin Meillassoux, *The Number and the Siren: A Decipherment of Mallarmé's Coup de Dés*, trans. Robin MacKay (Falmouth; New York: Urbanomic; Sequence Press, 2012), 216.

121 Ibid., 222.

122 She does this in terms of a critique of apparatus theory, Doane, *Femmes Fatales*, 79.

123 Laura Marks, *Touch: Sensuous Theory and Multisensory Media* (Minneapolis; London: University of Minnesota Press, 2002), 13.

124 Ibid., 77.

125 Qtd. in Sergei Eisenstein, *Film Form: Essay in Film Theory*, ed. and trans. Jay Leyda (San Diego: Harcourt, Inc., 1977), 213.

126 Another way to say it is that what makes this passage from Dickens erotic is the way in which the image of the tumbril carries both wine and "absolute monarchs."

127 Steven Shaviro, *The Cinematic Body* (Minneapolis; London: University of Minnesota Press, 1993), 57.

128 Ibid.

129 Jalufka and Koeberl, "Moonstruck," 191.

130 *Nude* was filmed at Ed Leedskalnin's Coral Castle near Homestead, Florida; see Rusty McClure and Jack Heffron,

Coral Castle: The Mystery of Ed Leedskalnin and his American Stonehenge (Covington: Clerisy Press, 2009).

131 David Allyn, Make *Love, Not War: The Sexual Revolution: An Unfettered History* (New York: Little, Brown and Company, 2000), 24-5.

132 Although in Europe nudism has a long tradition of being political. See Richard Cleminson, "Medical Understandings of the Body: 1750 to the Present," in *The Routledge History of Sex and the Body: 1500 to the Present*, eds. Sarah Toulalan and Kate Fisher (Oxon: Routledge, 2013), 84. For a wider historical and philosophical perspective, see Giorgio Agamben, "Nudity," in *Nudities*, trans. David Kishik and Stefan Pedatella (Stanford: Stanford University Press, 2011).

133 Mike Watt, *Fervid Filmmaking: 66 Cult Pictures of Vision, Verve and No Self-Restraint* (Jefferson: McFarland, 2013), 160. On the legality of Wishman's productions, see Tania Modleski, "Women's Cinema as Counterphobic Cinema: Doris Wishman as the Last Auteur," in *Sleaze Artists: Cinema at the Margins of Taste, Style and Politics*, ed. Jeffery Sconce (Durham: Duke, 2007), 49.

134 Although Marie Lathers sees a more sexual suggestion: "Although these 'noble savages' are innocent in that they are nude but do not seemingly engage in sexual activity, the facts that the women look vaguely like porn stars and that Cathy the secretary is clearly up to no good suggest a fantasy of wild savage sex in space," *Space Oddities*, 167.

135 Shaviro, *The Cinematic Body*, 142-3.

136 Ross, "Uses of Camp," 67.

137 Agamben, "Nudity," 55.

138 Ibid., 65.

139 See Roberta Smith, "Critic's Notebook: Standing and Staring, Yet Aiming for Empowerment," *The New York Times* (May 6, 1998): E2.

140 Which would fall in line with Lathers' reading where "In

the end, Jeff must leave the earth to recognize gender difference among humans, and topless women with butt cleavage reveal this to him," *Space Oddities*, 167.

141 Harman, *Quentin Meillassoux*, 156. This is Harman's main argument in *Weird Realism*, that "reality is not made of statements," 14.

142 A. Bowdoin Van Riper, *Rockets and Missiles: The Life Story of a Technology* (Baltimore: John Hopkins University Press, 2007), 93.

143 M. Keith Booker, *Alternate Americas: Science Fiction Film and American Culture* (Westport: Praeger Publishers, 2006), 4.

144 George Mann, *The Mammoth Encyclopedia of Science Fiction* (New York: Carroll & Graf Publishers, 2001), 356.

145 Vivian Sobchack, *Screening Space: The American Science Fiction Film* (New Brunswick: Rutgers, 2001), 22.

146 Samuel Weber, *Theatricality as Medium* (New York: Fordham University Press, 2004), 98.

147 Harman, *Wierd Realism*, 242.

148 Germaine Dulac, "The Expressive Techniques of the Cinema," in *French Film Theory and Criticism: 1907-1959, Volume 1 1907-1929*, ed. Richard Abel (Princeton: Princeton University Press, 1988), 311.

149 Henri Bergson, *Creative Evolution*, trans. Arthur Mitchell (Lanham: University Press of America, 1983), 1.

150 Ibid., 2.

151 Ibid., 7.

152 Ibid., 11.

153 Gilles Deleuze, *Cinema 1: The Movement-Image*, trans. Hugh Tomlinson and Barbara Habberjam (Minneapolis: University of Minnesota Press, 2006), 1.

154 Ibid., 22.

155 Mullarkey, *Philosophy of the Moving Image*, 89.

156 Bergson, *Creative Evolution*, 305-6.

157 Christian Metz, *Film Language: A Semiotics of the Cinema*,

trans. Michael Taylor (Chicago: University of Chicago Press, 1991), 24-8.

158 Brunner claims that "Destination Moon includes an inventive comic-strip sequence dismissing the 'comic book stuff' characteristic of most depictions of moon flight," *Moon*, 215.

159 Jalufka and Koeberl, "Moonstruck," 185.

160 Robert Kolker, *A Cinema of Loneliness* (New York: Oxford University Press, 2001), 361.

161 Robert Altman, *Interviews* (Jackson: University Press of Mississippi, 2000), 140.

162 Robert Self, *Robert Altman's Subliminal Reality* (Minneapolis: University of Minnesota Press, 2002), 27-8.

163 Alain Badiou, *The Handbook of Inaesthetics,* trans. Alberto Toscano (Stanford: Stanford University Press, 2005), 78.

164 Mullarkey, *Philosophy of the Moving Image,* 129.

165 Badiou, *Handbook,* 78.

166 Alain Badiou, *Being and Event,* trans. Oliver Feltham (London; New York: Continuum, 2005), 177. For example, Badiou describes "the Hayden event" as "a wholly new architectronic and thematic principle, a new way of developing musical writing from the basis of a few transformable units—which was precisely what, from within the baroque style, could not be perceived (there could be no knowledge of it)," *Ethics: An Essay on the Understanding of Evil,* trans. Peter Hallward (London; New York: Verso, 2001), 68-9.

167 Badiou, *Handbook,* 83.

168 Jacques Rancière, "Aesthetics, Inaesthetics, Anti-Aesthetics," in *Think Again: Alain Badiou and the Future of Philosophy,* ed. Peter Hallward (London; New York: Continuum, 2004), 229.

169 Peter Hallward, "Translator's Introduction," in *Badiou, Ethics: An Essay on the Understanding of Evil,* trans. Peter Hallward (London; New York: Verso, 2001), xi.

170 Alain Badiou, *Saint Paul: The Foundation of Universalism*, trans. Ray Brassier (Stanford: Stanford University Press, 2003), 87-8.

171 Alain Badiou, *In Praise of Love*, trans. Peter Bush (New York: The New Press, 2009), 42.

172 Ibid., 44.

173 Ibid., 38.

174 Barry Keith Grant, "Of Men and Monoliths: Science Fiction, Gender, and 2001: A Space Odyssey," in *Stanley Kubrick's 2001: A Space Odyssey: New Essays*, ed. Robert Kolker (Oxford: Oxford University Press, 2006), 76.

175 Kevin Decker, "Kockout! Killer's Kiss, the Somatic, and Kubrick," in *The Philosophy of Stanley Kubrick*, ed. Jerold Abrams (Lexington: The University Press of Kentucky, 2007), 99.

176 Mario Falsetto, *Stanley Kubrick: A Narrative and Stylistic Analysis* (Westport: Greenwood Publishing Group, 2001), xviii.

177 Martin Heidegger, *Being and Time*, trans. Joan Stambaugh (Albany: State University of New York Press, 1996), 64.

178 Ibid., 67.

179 Ibid., 68.

180 Graham Harman, *Tool-Being: Heidegger and the Metaphysics of Objects* (Peru: Open Court, 2002), 49.

181 In a well-known Playboy interview Kubrick asks "How much would we appreciate La Gioconda today if Leonardo had written at the bottom of the canvas: 'This lady is smiling slightly because she has rotten teeth'—or 'because she's hiding a secret from her lover'? It would shut off the viewer's appreciation and shackle him to a 'reality' other than his own. I don't want that to happen to 2001," Eric Nordern, "Playboy Interview: Stanley Kubrick," in *Stanley Kubrick Interviews*, ed. Gene Phillips (Jackson: University Press of Mississippi, 2001), 48.

182 Arthur C. Clarke, "The Sentinel," in *The Nine Billion Names of God: The Best Short Stories of Arthur C. Clarke* (Harcourt, Brace and World, 1967), 268.

183 Quentin Meillassoux, *The Divine Inexistence,* in Graham Harman, *Quentin Meillassoux: Philosophy in the Making* (Edinburgh: University of Edinburgh Press, 2011), 189.

184 However, while non-life does not contain life, there are pre-conditions for life, such as the age and size of the universe, as John Barrow explains: "Complex living things like ourselves must be made from elements like carbon, nitrogen and oxygen. These elements are produced by a process of nuclear alchemy inside the stars. Over billions of years hydrogen and helium gases are burnt into carbon, nitrogen and oxygen. The stars explode and distribute the elements of life through space. Eventually they end up in you and me. So any Universe containing the building blocks required for the evolution of biological complexity must be billions of years old. Remarkably, since the Universe is expanding, this also means that Universes that contain life must be billions of light years in size. You do, indeed, need 'world enough and time' to think about the Universe after all," *Between Inner Space and Outer Space: Essays on Science, Art and Philosophy* (Oxford: Oxford University Press, 2000), 178.

185 Meillassoux, *Divine Inexistence,* 192.

186 Ibid., 192.

187 Ibid., 175.

188 Ibid., 176.

189 Here Badiou locates his key difference from Meillassoux, which is that he does not see how randomness can be co-opted into what Meillassoux terms contingency, see Alain Badiou, Joël Bellassen and Lous Mossot, *The Rational Kernel of the Hegelian Dialectic: Translations, Introductions and Commentary on a Text by Zhang Shiying,* trans and ed.

Tzuchien Tho (Melbourne: Re.Press, 2011), 93-4.

190 Meillassoux, Quentin, Florian Hecker and Robin Mackay, "Chez Meillassoux, Paris, 22.7.2010," *Urbanomic Documents* UF13-1/2 (2010), Internet: http://www.urbanomic.com/event-uf13-details.php.

191 Ibid.

192 Ibid.

193 The interview used here also deals with sound as if part of a collaboration between Meillassoux and musician Florian Hecker.

194 Qtd. in Andrew Chaikin, "Live from the Moon: The Societal Impact of Apollo," in Steven Dick and Roger Lanunius, eds, *Societal Impact of Spaceflight* (Washington D.C.: NASA, 2007), 55. Chaikin's book *A Man on the Moon: The Voyages of the Apollo Astronauts* (New York; London: Penguin, 1998) was adapted into the HBO mini-series *From the Earth to the Moon* (1998), discussed below.

195 TMA stands for Tycho Magnetic Anomaly and is the name given to the monolith in the moon. Tycho is the name of a large lunar crater.

196 Which Chion calls "the most moving *acousmêtre* death in cinema," *The Voice in Cinema,* trans. Claudia Gorbman (New York: Columbia University Press, 1999), 45.

197 Ibid.

198 However, a different trajectory is taken regarding the monolith on the moon than the one Chion chooses in his monograph on the film where he states that "The monolith is a symbol of burial: one of the rare things we find out about the one found on the moon is that it was 'deliberately buried'. It is exhumed as if it were some sort of pharaonic sarcophagus. This refers back to funerary symbolism...", *Kubrick's Cinema Odyssey,* trans. Claudia Gorbman (London: British Film Institute, 2001), 143.

199 Ibid., 21.

200 Jalufka and Koeberl, "Moonstruck," 198.

201 Ibid., 200.

202 Paolo Ulivi, Lunar *Exploration: Human Pioneers and Robotic Surveyors* (New York: Springer, 2004), 26-8.

203 Shaviro, *Post Cinematic Affect*, 139.

204 This is similar to current debates regarding "monoliths" found in images of Mars.

205 In an interview issued around the time of the film's remastering onto DVD, Kamecke said that "When I went down to Cape Canaveral in Florida to scout the location, I was shown the giant crawler that moves the rocket to the launch pad. It was as big as a football field. ... What came to mind was Stonehenge. The year before I had been there and I thought, what an impractical thing for man to have done." It had parallels, he thought, with "putting three of our species into space and walking on the Moon," Alison Gibson, "Moonwalk One," *Mid-Day* 7.19.2009, Internet: http://www.mid-day.com/specials/2009/jul/190709-Moonwalk-One-Apollo-13-lost-films-space-launch-Play.htm.

206 Stuart Miles, "Moonwalk One: Documenting the Moon Landing," *Pocket-Lint* (7.14.2009) Internet: http://www.pocket-lint.com/news/96833-moonwalk-one-dvd-theo-kamecke.

207 A similar sequence is found at the beginning of Godfrey Reggio's *Koyaanisqatsi* (1982).

208 Curt Cloninger, "Manifesto for a Theory of the 'New Aesthetic,'" *Mute* (10.3.2012) Internet: http://www.metamute.org/editorial/articles/manifesto-theory-%E2%80%98new-aesthetic%E2%80%99.

209 Stephen Glantz, "The Making of 'Moonwalk,'" *Filmmakers Newsletter* 6:9/10 (Summer 1973), 29.

210 Bruce Sterling, "An Essay on the New Aesthetic," *Beyond the Beyond* (6.2.2012) Internet: http://www.wired.com/beyond

_the_beyond/2012/04/an-essay-on-the-new-aesthetic/.
211 Cloninger, "Manifesto."
212 Ibid.
213 Heidegger, *Being and Time*, 68.
214 Christopher Fynsk does much work to show how in Heidegger "use" is developed in the way that truth "uses" a human in order to come forth in his chapter "The Free Use of the Proper" in *Language and Relation... that there is language* (Stanford: Stanford University Press, 1996), esp. 130-1.
215 Harman, *Tool-Being*, 16.
216 Ibid.
217 This fuzziness is not a product of the camera, which sent relatively clear pictures that the NASA engineers saw in real time but rather that the footage was transmitted at 500 kHz while the commercial TV industry of the time used 4.5 MHz. While the original broadcast was recorded by NASA the tapes were recorded over. For a history of these recordings see NASA, *The Apollo 11 Telemetry Data Recordings: A Final Report* (2009), Internet: http://www.honeysucklecreek.net/Apollo_11/tapes/Apollo_11_TV_Tapes_Report.pdf.
218 For example, in reference to a gun or police uniform in Katheryn Bigelow's *Blue Steel* (1989), Shaviro, *The Cinematic Body*, 4.
219 Martin Heidegger, "The Question Concerning Technology," in *Basic Writings*, ed. David Farrell Krell (New York: HarperCollins Publishers, 1993), 311.
220 Ibid., 319.
221 Ibid., 320.
222 Ibid., 324.
223 Ibid., 320.
224 Ibid., 325.
225 Of course Heidegger's thought is ugly and dangerous in another manner for at the same time he notoriously claimed that the bomb at Hiroshima was not particularly important

(because the real disaster of technology had already happened) and he equated mechanized agriculture with concentration camps. As Fynsk has suggested this aspect of Heidegger "points to the limits of Heidegger's conception of authentic death," *Heidegger: Thought and History, Expanded Edition* (Ithaca: Cornell University Press, 1993), 245n.21. See Harman, "Technology, Objects and Things in Heidegger," *Cambridge Journal of Economics* 34 (2010), 22.

226 Heidegger, "The Question Concerning Technology," 333.

227 Ibid., 337.

228 Ibid., 338.

229 See Jacques Derrida, *Of Spirit: Heidegger and the Question*, trans. Geoffrey Bennington and Rachel Bowlby (Chicago: The University of Chicago Press, 1987), 129-136n5.

230 Harman, "Technology," 21.

231 I have followed this train of thought previously by locating Heidegger's "proper" relation toward death within his description of an impoverished relation to the world in *Facticity, Poverty and Clones: On Kazuo Ishiguro's* Never Let Me Go (New York; Dresden: Atropos Press, 2010), 107-129.

232 Harman, "Technology," 23.

233 Colleen Boyle, "You Saw the Whole of the Moon: The Role of Imagination in the Perceptual Construction of the Moon," *Leonardo* 46:3 (2013): 246-252.

234 Such legitimization is also seen at the end of the episode when the actual footage is allowed to be presented on its own, without any reenacted intervention.

235 Harman, "Technology," 24.

236 Sherryl Vint, *Science Fiction* (London: Bloomsbury, 2014), 27-8. In addition, as Mark Rose argues, much as reenacted footage is seen to be more "truthful" than actual, science fiction is about "implying credibility by invoking the incredible," *Alien Encounters: Anatomy of Science Fiction* (Cambridge; London: Harvard University Press, 1981), 25.

237 Heidegger, "The Question," 329.

238 François Bucher, "Subjects of the American Moon: From Studio as Reality to Reality as Studio," *e-flux* 9 (2009), Internet: www.eflux.com/journal/subjects-of-the-american-moon-from-studio-as-reality-to-reality-as-studio/. In a classic text Douglas Davis describes the early attempts at video art as distinctive because of their being "deliberately crude in form and intimate in contact," *Art and the Future: A History/Prophecy of the Collaboration between Science, Technology and Art* (New York: Praeger Publishers, 1973), 86.

239 Meillassoux, *The Number*, 146.

240 Harman also highlights the hesitant aspect of Lovecraft's work as the defining stylistic element: "Not even Poe gives us such hesitant narrators, wavering so uncertainly as to whether their coming words can do justice to the unspeakable reality they confront," *Wierd Realism*, 10.

241 Marks, *Touch*, 8.

242 Anne Friedberg, "The End of Cinema: Multimedia and the Technological Change," in Christine Gledhill and Linda Williams, eds., *Reinventing Film Studies* (New York: Oxford University Press, 2000), 442.

243 Paul Virilio, "The Third Window: An Interview with Paul Virilio," in Cynthia Schneider and Brian Wallis, eds., *Global Television* (Cambridge: MIT Press, 1998), 187.

244 The last words Collier speaks in the film are: "I want to thank Frank Hughes, who gave freely of his time, and curator Alan Ridell, who did not."

245 Friedberg, "End of Cinema," 444.

246 Avital Ronell, "Trauma TV: Twelve Steps Beyond the Pleasure Principle," *The ÜberReader*, ed. Diane Davis (Urbana; Chicago: University of Illinois Press, 2008), 76.

247 Ibid., 78.

248 Ibid., 85.

249 Paul Virilio, *The Information Bomb*, trans. Chris Turner

(London; New York: Verso, 2005), 80.

250 Siegfried Zielinksi, *Audiovisions: Cinema and Television as* Entr'actes *in History*, trans. Gloria Custance (Amsterdam: Amsterdam University Press, 1999), 240.

251 This is important because Harman excludes cinema from a horizontal tension, *Wierd Realism*, 24.

252 Matt Strassler, "TIME for a Little Soul-Searching," *Of Particular Significance* (Dec 3, 2012), Internet: www.profmattstrassler.com/2012/12/03/time-for-soul-searchin/.

253 This idea is taken from the first developed conspiracy theory about the moon landings, Bill Kaysing's *We Never Went to the Moon: Americas Thirty Billion Dollar Swindle!* (Fountain Valley, Eden Press, 1976). Roger Launius, fom the Smithsonian Institute, has prepared a detailed overview of the history and context of culture surrounding those trying to prove the moon landing was a hoax, see "Denying the Apollo Moon Landings: Conspiracy and Questioning in Modern American History," delivered as a part of the Smithsonian's Apollo Space Program online conference, November 10, 2009, Internet: http://www.smithsonianconference.org/apollo/

254 Walter Ong, *Orality and Literacy: The Technologizing of the World* (London; New York: Routledge, 2013).

255 Slavoj Žižek, *Enjoy Your Symptom!: Jacques Lacan in Hollywood and Out* (New York; London: Routledge, 2008), 38.

256 Levi Bryant, *The Democracy of Objects* (Ann Arbor: Open Humanities Press, 2011), 246.

257 Ibid., 19.

258 Jacques Rancière, *The Future of the Image*, trans. Gregory Elliott (New York; London: Verso, 2003), 3.

259 While Sander Lee reads the lunar scene as how "Isaac and Mary, appearing as small figures walking in the distance, seem to have left this world, their conversation detached

from earthly reality," *Woody Allen's Angst: Philosophical Commentaries on his Serious Films* (Jefferson: McFarland, 1997), 97, in fact they are very much on an unfantastic Earth, for not only does the film lack any pretensions to science fiction, but the lunar diorama is interesting as a diorama and not as a location of otherworldly detachment. Yet at the same time this image of the moon is the context in which a new relationship can develop, that between Isaac and Mary. Thus Manhattan has some similarities to "Breakaway" in that in both new forms of understanding come out of a new way of relating to the moon as an image rather than about anything strange taking place on its surface.

260 Douglas Brode, *The Films of Woody Allen* (New York: Carol Publishing Group, 1991), 186.

261 Jane Roscoe and Craig Hight, *Faking It: Mock-Documentary and the Subversion of Factuality* (Manchester: Manchester University Press, 2001), 73.

262 Ibid., 185.

263 David Bordwell, "Camera Movement and Cinematic Space," in *Explorations in Film Theory: Selected Essays From Ciné-Tracts*, Ron Burnett, ed. (Bloomington: Indiana University Press, 1991).

264 Graham Harman, *Bells and Whistles: More Speculative Realism*, (Hants: Zero Books, 2013), 66.

265 Rose, *Alien Encounters*, 95.

266 Istvan Csicsery-Ronay, Jr., *The Seven Beauties of Science Fiction* (Middletown: Wesleyan University Press, 2008), 59-60.

267 Caetin Benson-Allott, *Killer Tapes and Shattered Screens: Video Spectatorship from VHS to File Sharing* (Berkeley: University of California Press, 2013), 255n59.

268 Although this technique garnered praise for Fodorchenko's film, it has mainly caused derision in regard to *Apollo 18*, leading to commentators calling it "disappointing," Gerald

Alva Miller, *Exploring the Limits of the Human through Science Fiction* (New York: Palgrave Macmillan, 2012), 159, and "80 minutes of dead air," David Edelstein, "Movie Review: Apollo 18 Gets Lost in Space," *Vulture* (2011), Internet: http://www.vulture.com/2011/09/apollo_18_review.html.

269 In fact there is another film about the moon which, in part, features fake found footage, William Karel's 2002 *Opération Lune/The Dark Side of the Moon,* although this film creates more of a "vertical" tension by featuring interviews with real-world figures such as Donald Rumsfeld, Henry Kissinger and Buzz Aldrin.

270 Marks, *Touch,* 8.

271 Ibid. Here Marks is speaking of the work of Atom Egoyan.

272 Harman, *Weird Realism,* 27.

273 Ron Sorensen, *Seeing Dark Things: The Philosophy of Shadows* (Oxford; New York: Oxford University Press, 2008), 60-4.

274 Ibid., 65.

275 Ibid.

276 Shaviro, *The Cinematic Body,* 43.

277 Manuel DeLanda, *Intensive Science and Virtual Philosophy* (London; New York: Continuum, 2004), 58.

278 Ibid. DeLanda then uses this equality of scales to trace the development from individual to cities and nations in *A New Philosophy of Society: Assemblage Theory and Social Complexity* (London; New York: Continuum, 2006).

279 Eugene Thacker, *In the Dust of This Planet: Horror of Philosophy Vol 1* (Hants: Zero Books, 2011), 12.

280 Ibid., 15.

281 Ibid., 20.

282 Ibid., 17.

283 Harman, *Circus Philosophicus,* 73.

284 Thacker, *In the Dust,* 6-7.

285 Timothy Morton, *Hyperobjects: Philosophy and Ecology at the End of the World* (Minneapolis; London, University of

Minnesota Press, 2013), 128.

286 Morton, *Hyperobjects*, 128.

287 Thomas Piketty calls for a similar planetary scale in looking at changes in the forms and use of capital, saying that a minimum 200-year span is needed to see changes which are too slow for a single generation to observe, *Capital in the Twenty-First Century*, trans. Arthur Goldhammer (Cambridge; London, The Belknap Press of Harvard University Press, 2014), 74-7.

288 Harman, *Weird Realism*, 34.

zero books

Contemporary culture has eliminated both the concept of the public and the figure of the intellectual. Former public spaces – both physical and cultural – are now either derelict or colonized by advertising. A cretinous anti-intellectualism presides, cheerled by expensively educated hacks in the pay of multinational corporations who reassure their bored readers that there is no need to rouse themselves from their interpassive stupor. The informal censorship internalized and propagated by the cultural workers of late capitalism generates a banal conformity that the propaganda chiefs of Stalinism could only ever have dreamt of imposing. Zer0 Books knows that another kind of discourse – intellectual without being academic, popular without being populist – is not only possible: it is already flourishing, in the regions beyond the striplit malls of so-called mass media and the neurotically bureaucratic halls of the academy. Zer0 is committed to the idea of publishing as a making public of the intellectual. It is convinced that in the unthinking, blandly consensual culture in which we live, critical and engaged theoretical reflection is more important than ever before.

ZERO BOOKS

If this book has helped you to clarify an idea, solve a problem or extend your knowledge, you may like to read more titles from Zero Books. Recent bestsellers are:

Capitalist Realism Is there no alternative?
Mark Fisher
An analysis of the ways in which capitalism has presented itself as the only realistic political-economic system.
Paperback: November 27, 2009 978-1-84694-317-1 $14.95 £7.99.
eBook: July 1, 2012 978-1-78099-734-6 $9.99 £6.99.

The Wandering Who? A study of Jewish identity politics
Gilad Atzmon
An explosive unique crucial book tackling the issues of Jewish Identity Politics and ideology and their global influence.
Paperback: September 30, 2011 978-1-84694-875-6 $14.95 £8.99.
eBook: September 30, 2011 978-1-84694-876-3 $9.99 £6.99.

Clampdown Pop-cultural wars on class and gender
Rhian E. Jones
Class and gender in Britpop and after, and why 'chav' is a feminist issue.
Paperback: March 29, 2013 978-1-78099-708-7 $14.95 £9.99.
eBook: March 29, 2013 978-1-78099-707-0 $7.99 £4.99.

The Quadruple Object
Graham Harman
Uses a pack of playing cards to present Harman's metaphysical system of fourfold objects, including human access, Heidegger's indirect causation, panpsychism and ontography.
Paperback: July 29, 2011 978-1-84694-700-1 $16.95 £9.99.

Weird Realism Lovecraft and Philosophy
Graham Harman
As Hölderlin was to Martin Heidegger and Mallarmé to Jacques Derrida, so is H.P. Lovecraft to the Speculative Realist philosophers.
Paperback: September 28, 2012 978-1-78099-252-5 $24.95 £14.99.
eBook: September 28, 2012 978-1-78099-907-4 $9.99 £6.99.

Sweetening the Pill or How We Got Hooked on Hormonal Birth Control
Holly Grigg-Spall
Is it really true? Has contraception liberated or oppressed women?
Paperback: September 27, 2013 978-1-78099-607-3 $22.95 £12.99.
eBook: September 27, 2013 978-1-78099-608-0 $9.99 £6.99.

Why Are We The Good Guys? Reclaiming Your Mind From The Delusions Of Propaganda
David Cromwell
A provocative challenge to the standard ideology that Western power is a benevolent force in the world.
Paperback: September 28, 2012 978-1-78099-365-2 $26.95 £15.99.
eBook: September 28, 2012 978-1-78099-366-9 $9.99 £6.99.

The Truth about Art Reclaiming quality
Patrick Doorly
The book traces the multiple meanings of art to their various sources, and equips the reader to choose between them.
Paperback: August 30, 2013 978-1-78099-841-1 $32.95 £19.99.

Bells and Whistles More Speculative Realism
Graham Harman
In this diverse collection of sixteen essays, lectures, and interviews Graham Harman lucidly explains the principles of

Speculative Realism, including his own object-oriented philosophy.
Paperback: November 29, 2013 978-1-78279-038-9 $26.95 £15.99.
eBook: November 29, 2013 978-1-78279-037-2 $9.99 £6.99.

Towards Speculative Realism: Essays and Lectures Essays and Lectures
Graham Harman
These writings chart Harman's rise from Chicago sportswriter to co founder of one of Europe's most promising philosophical movements: Speculative Realism.
Paperback: November 26, 2010 978-1-84694-394-2 $16.95 £9.99.
eBook: January 1, 1970 978-1-84694-603-5 $9.99 £6.99.

Meat Market Female flesh under capitalism
Laurie Penny
A feminist dissection of women's bodies as the fleshy fulcrum of capitalist cannibalism, whereby women are both consumers and consumed.
Paperback: April 29, 2011 978-1-84694-521-2 $12.95 £6.99.
eBook: May 21, 2012 978-1-84694-782-7 $9.99 £6.99.

Translating Anarchy The Anarchism of Occupy Wall Street
Mark Bray
An insider's account of the anarchists who ignited Occupy Wall Street.
Paperback: September 27, 2013 978-1-78279-126-3 $26.95 £15.99.
eBook: September 27, 2013 978-1-78279-125-6 $6.99 £4.99.

One Dimensional Woman
Nina Power
Exposes the dark heart of contemporary cultural life by examining pornography, consumer capitalism and the ideology of women's work.

Paperback: November 27, 2009 978-1-84694-241-9 $14.95 £7.99.
eBook: July 1, 2012 978-1-78099-737-7 $9.99 £6.99.

Dead Man Working
Carl Cederstrom, Peter Fleming
An analysis of the dead man working and the way in which capital is now colonizing life itself.
Paperback: May 25, 2012 978-1-78099-156-6 $14.95 £9.99.
eBook: June 27, 2012 978-1-78099-157-3 $9.99 £6.99.

Unpatriotic History of the Second World War
James Heartfield
The Second World War was not the Good War of legend. James Heartfield explains that both Allies and Axis powers fought for the same goals - territory, markets and natural resources.
Paperback: September 28, 2012 978-1-78099-378-2 $42.95 £23.99.
eBook: September 28, 2012 978-1-78099-379-9 $9.99 £6.99.

Find more titles at www.zero-books.net